COMPTON, KERN, TRUCKEE & WEED

California Places Named For People

Steven Gilbar

INTRODUCTION

This little volume couples my interests in California geography and in eponyms by telling the stories of the men and women who gave their names to places in the state. There are books about California place names. They are long scholarly tomes with very brief etymologies of places, be they named after people or things or other places. Here you will find only "named" locales, be it the surname, first name, or middle name of a person. This book is arranged alphabetically, but not by place name, but by the name of the person who gave the place its name. So, for example, Mount Clarence King is not found under "M" but "K" and Santa Monica is listed under "M" rather than "S." I have included all counties and cities and state parks that are named for people. After that I have selected from the thousands of place names--rivers and creeks, lakes and mountains, towns and villages, passes and military bases--those that are interesting, admittedly an arbitrary and subjective undertaking. My intent is to inform and entertain. The stories of the Spaniards, scouts, and senators, the settlers, sea-captains, and saints, the sinners, scholars and squatters whose names dot the California map combine to form a mosaic history of the Golden State.

A

ADAMS, MOUNT ANSEL

The 11,760-foot remote peak stands at the headwaters of the Lyell Fork of the Merced River, on the border of Yosemite National Park. In 1985 the U.S. Geological Survey (USGS) demarked the mountain for Ansel Adams (1902-1984), the San Francisco-born landscape photographer revered for his dramatic black-and-white images of Yosemite and the Sierra Nevada. Adams, a member of the Sierra Club since his youth, spending many summers on backcountry journeys with the club, had first climbed and photographed the peak when he was nineteen. Years later, the club informally named the mountain for him, but the rules of the U.S. Board of Geographical Names (a division of the USGS) did not permit names of living persons to be used. So approval had to await more than fifty years until after Adam's death. The same year, in further commemoration of the photographer's legacy, Congress renamed the Minarets Wilderness in the Inyo National Forest, and contiguous with Yosemite, the **Ansel Adams Wilderness Area**.

AGASSIZ, MOUNT

The name Louis Agassiz (1807-1873) has all but melted into the mists of history. Yet, at a time when geology was the country's trendiest science, Agassiz, who taught the subject at Harvard for many years after emigrating from his native Switzerland, was probably its most renowned theorist. His belief that the laws of embryonic development (ontogeny) are also the laws of geological succession (phylogeny) was used by Darwin in fashioning his theory of evolution by natural selection. Ironically, Agassiz opposed Darwin's conclusion, believing that new species could emerge only through divine intervention.

In 1879 an explorer/mountaineer with the curious name of Lilbourne Alsip Winchell (1855-1939) gave the name "Agassiz Needle" to the 13,898-foot "giant mass" at the northwest end of the Palisades of the Sierra Nevada. Alas, the man mistook his mountain, for it seems that he was referring to a more needle-like, less lofty, peak, what is now called Mount Winchell (named not for him, but for a cousin, Alexander Winchell [1824-1891], a prominent professor of geology at the University of Michigan at that time), about a half-mile southeast. The name was officially changed from the non-descriptive "Agassiz Needle" to "Mount Agassiz" in the 1930's at the request of the Sierra Club.

AGOURA

The Los Angeles County town began as the dusty stagecoach stop of Vejar Junction. In the 1920s, after Paramount Studios bought a nearby ranch to shoot Westerns, the community was known briefly as "Picture City." In 1928 a group of residents formed a Chamber of Commerce which petitioned to have a permanent post office established there. The postal authorities replied that the petitioners would have to submit ten potential one-word names for the town. One name tendered was "Agoure," for one of the area's colorful early landowners, Pierre Agoure (1854-1912). Though French by birth, he favored Spanish dress and adopted the name of "Don Pedro Agoure." At seventeen he had come to California's

6

Conejo Valley to work as a sheep herder. By the time he was twenty-one he had begun his own sheep-raising venture, starting with four-hundred head, adding to his holdings until he had over 25,000, making him one of the most successful stockmen of the region. By 1906, he owned almost 17,000 acres of grazing land.

How the "e" of "Agoure" became "a" remains an unsettled issue. Some believe it was done intentionally for ease of spelling; others claim postal officials simply misspelled it. In either event, the name was selected. In 1982 most of the still unincorporated Agoura split off and became the city of **Agoura Hills**.

ALBANY

Adjacent to Berkeley, the city was named for the hometown of Frank Roberts, its first mayor: Albany, New York. It, in turn, was named in 1664 in honor of the son of Charles II of England, James, then the Duke of Albany (1633-1701), who would succeed to the throne in 1685 as King James II.

Allen Allensworth

ALLENSWORTH STATE HISTORIC PARK, COL.

Allen Allensworth (1842-1914) was by all accounts a remarkable man. He is credited with founding the only California town to be established, financed and governed

7

by African Americans. Born into slavery, Allensworth escaped during the Civil War and served in the Union Army. In 1871 he became a minister and in 1886 accepted a commission as a chaplain of the all-black 24th Army Infantry. Upon his retirement twenty years later, he held the rank of lieutenant-colonel, making him the highest ranking black officer of the time. He then decided to join in an effort to create a self-governed town for black people. In 1908 the group incorporated the California Colony and Home Protection Association and chose a site north of Bakersfield off Highway 99. The new town grew rapidly as enterprising black men and women purchased lots, started farms and built homes. In a short time the town had a school, church, library, and post office. Unfortunately, within a few years, due to circumstances beyond its control, including a drop in the area's water table, the closure of its railroad station, and the death of Allensworth, the once-prosperous town withered. But it remains for many a pioneering effort in black self-determination. In 1974 the hamlet came back to life as a state historic park.

ALMANOR, LAKE
The Plumas County lake was created when the first hydroelectric dam on the Feather River was completed in 1917. It was named after the daughters of the man who was chiefly responsible for its construction, Guy Earl, who headed the Great Western Power Company. Their names were ALice, MARtha, and EleaNOR.

AMADOR COUNTY/VALLEY
The son of a Spanish soldier who had settled in California in 1771, José María Amador (1794-1883) was born at his father's post, the San Francisco Presidio, He spent his early years in the Mexican army as a soldier, explorer, and Indian fighter and was later administrator at Mission San José. As a reward for his service, in 1834 he was granted 18,000 acres of land—*Rancho San Ramón*—in the San Francisco-Oakland Bay area. There he raised cattle, horses, grapes and grain and where his name is preserved in

"Amador Valley" near present-day Pleasanton. In 1848 he and several of his Native American workers left the ranch for the gold fields, establishing a successful mining camp along a creek in the Sierra Nevada foothills, about forty-five miles southeast of Sacramento. That creek became known as "Amador's Creek" and, soon after, camps called "Amador Crossing," and "South Amador" were founded and became what is today **Amador City**, the smallest incorporated city, by area, in California at 0.3 square miles. In 1854, when legislation dividing Calaveras County was debated, a motion to name the new county after Amador instead of George Washington, as one faction had moved, was adopted. It became the first and, to this day, only county in the state named for a native Californian.

ANA, SANTA

The seat of Orange County honors Saint Anne, the traditional name for the mother of the Virgin Mary. *El Vallejo de Santa Ana* was the name given the river and valley after its discovery by Gaspar de Portolá on her feast day in 1769. José Antonio Yorba, a young soldier in Portolá's party, and his nephew Juan Peralta, were given the land grant, the only one ever granted under Spanish rule. They developed the *Rancho Santiago de Santa Ana* for cattle grazing and farming. In 1869, William H. Spurgeon bought 70 acres from them and plotted a site for a town, to be called "Santa Ana."

The diminutive of "Ana," "Anita," is found in several places, but it is not a separate saint—there is no "Saint Annie." *Rancho Santa Anita*—which became the site of the Santa Anita Racetrack in Arcadia—is named for Anita Cota, the fiancé of its owner, Claudio Lopez, mayordomo of San Gabriel Mission in the early 1800s.

ANAHEIM

The Orange County city began in 1857 as a colony of German farmers and winemakers. The following year the stockholders met to decide on a name for the settlement. "Annaheim" (spelled until the following year with two "n's") narrowly beating out "Annagau." The name is a blend of "Ana," from the nearby Santa Ana River, and "heim," German for home. See *Ana, Santa*, above.

ANDERSON

Nestled at the northern end of the Central Valley along the Sacramento River, the Shasta County city is named for Elias Anderson (1817-1907), who bought the American Ranch in 1856 and granted a parcel of it to the Oregon and California Railroad for a train station that would grow into a town and bear his name.

ANDERSON MARSH STATE PARK

The thousand-acre Lake County park protects several habitats including freshwater marsh, oak woodland, grasslands and riparian woodland. It is named for John Sill Anderson (1833-1912), a Scottish immigrant who bought the land in 1885 and started a dairy; later his family switched to raising cattle on the ranch that his descendants continued until the 1960s. It became a state park in 1982.

ANDERSON VALLEY

First populated by a tribe of Coastal Pomos, the valley carved by the Navarro River en route to the Mendocino Coast was "discovered" in 1851 by a son of one Walter Anderson while he was trailing a wounded elk on a hunting expedition. From the top of the rise he saw a lush valley below. He told his family of his discovery. His father decided to move there with his family and was soon followed by a stream of white settlers and ultimately resulted in his name being given to the valley. Anderson left in 1858 after the death of his wife, selling his land for eighty head of oxen.

ANDREAS FAULT, SAN

Andreas is an alternative spelling of *Andres*, Spanish for "Andrew." The fault was named for the **San Andreas Valley** in San Mateo County, christened *Cañada de San Andres* by Fr. Francisco Palou in 1774 because it was named on the saint's feast day. Andrew was an apostle who, according to the Gospel of John, became, with his brother Simon (Saint Peter), a disciple of Jesus. After the crucifixion, he traveled to Greece to preach and was eventually arrested and crucified. **San Andreas** is also the name of the county seat of Calaveras County.

ANDRUS ISLAND
The reclamation of the 7000-acre island on the Sacramento River, about halfway between Rio Vista and Walnut Grove, began when George Andrus settled at its northern end in 1852 and began to farm.

ANGELS CAMP
Coming to California from their native Rhode Island to serve under Colonel John C. Frémont during the Mexican War, the brothers Henry and George Angel headed for the gold fields as soon as the conflict ended in 1848. Finding placer mining too arduous, Henry decided to open a trading post in Calaveras County to provision miners. The business succeeded, the settlement grew and was dubbed "Angels Trading Post," later shortened to "Angels Camp." Mark Twain was a frequent visitor and it was at the Angels Hotel bar in 1865 that he heard the tale of a man and his remarkable frog that he would later turn into the famous tale "The Celebrated Jumping Frog of Calaveras County" which helped launch his career. The town commemorates the story with its annual Jumping Frog Jubilee. In 1912 Angels Camp was incorporated as the City of Angels, though it is still called Angels Camp informally.

ANGEL ISLAND
The island off the coast of San Francisco is a shortened version of *La Isla de Nuestra Señora de los Angeles*, given in 1775 by the Spanish Lt. Juan Manuel de Ayala, following a practice then common among Catholic explorers of naming sites for the religious feast days nearest to the time of discovery. "Our Lady of the Angels" is one of the names for Mary, mother of Jesus. The island now constitutes **Angel Island State Park**.

ANGWIN

The forested village on Howell Mountain overlooking Napa Valley was named in 1874 for Edwin Angwin (1841-1918). He had immigrated to California from his native Cornwall, England about 1864. The following year he bought two hundred acres and opened the Angwin Resort. By the century's end he owned almost 1600 acres. In 1909 Angwin sold the property to the Seventh-day Adventist Church which founded Pacific Union College on the site.

ANNADEL STATE PARK

The land comprising the Sonoma County park was part of a 19,000-acre Mexican land grant. In the 1880s, sheep and cattle grazing gradually gave way to quarrying operations. There was great demand for cobblestone material when San Francisco and other west coast cities were being built and rebuilt after the 1906 earthquake. It was a major source of income to the Wymore and the Hutchinson families who were the principal owners of the land at that time. The park takes its name from one of the Hutchinson granddaughters, Annie Hutchinson; the area was once known as "Annie's Dell."

ANSELMO, SAN

The Marin County town is not named for the 11[th]century Archbishop of Canterbury, Saint Anselm. Rather, it comes from the *Cañada de Anselmo*, where it lies, which, in turn, was probably named for a baptized Native American, with the *San* being added at a later date, probably to conform to all the other *Sans* and *Santas* in the region.

ANTONIO, MOUNT SAN

With San Gorgonio and San Jacinto, it is one of the trio of saintly mountains overlooking Los Angeles. Probably the best known of them, the 10,064-foot peak—the highest in the San Gabriel Mountains--is commonly known as Mount Baldy. It is named for Saint Anthony of Padua (1195-1231), the most revered of the disciples of Saint Francis. The name is thought to have been given in 1841 by the owner of *Rancho San Antonio*, Antonio María Lugo, most likely on the saint's feast day in June.

12

Juan Batista de Anza

ANZA BORREGO DESERT STATE PARK

California's largest state park, located in the Colorado Desert, is named for explorer Juan Bautista de Anza (1735-1788), who crossed the region in 1774, and *borrego*, the Spanish name for the "bighorn sheep" that ranged there. The city of **Anza** in southern Riverside County is also named for him. In 1773 Anza, then captain of the Presidio of Tubac (south of present-day Tucson, Arizona), received orders from the Viceroy of New Spain to find an overland route from Sonora to California that was needed to supply the California missions and presidios, as well as to launch a strong colonizing effort in "Alta California" to counter the recent encroachments of other European nations, especially Russia and England. In 1774 Anza, Father Francisco Garcés, a small group of soldiers and servants, and a herd of about two hundred cattle and pack animals set off from Tubac. Three months later they arrived at Mission San Gabriel (near what is now Los Angeles), having successfully found a route through near waterless deserts and uncharted mountain passes. In 1775 Anza spearheaded another overland trek to northern California, leading to the founding of the presidio of San Francisco. Anza served as governor of New Mexico for the ten years preceding his death. The **Juan Bautista de Anza**

National Historic Trail traces the explorer's route.

APPLEGATE

The Placer County town was settled in 1849 by a surveyor by the name of Lisbon Applegate (1803-1875). As the little community grew it called itself Lisbon in his honor. By 1855 when it was of a size to warrant its own post office (the settler's son George serving as the first postmaster), the name became official. However, in the 1870s, after the death of Lisbon, the town officials decided to honor its founding family and renamed it Applegate.

ARBUCKLE

The community's namesake is Tacitus Ryland Arbuckle (1834-1900) who moved to California in 1853 from his native Missouri, crossing the plains on an oxen-driven wagon. Rather than prospecting for gold, he got a job at a ranch in Napa Valley, where he learned the rudiments of Western farming before striking out for himself, trying his hand in Sonoma and Mendocino counties before settling in 1866 in central Colusa County, where he bought 160 acres of land and laid out the town of Arbuckle. When in 1875 the railroad proposed to lay line through this section, he gave it the right of way as well as land for a depot and sidings. He was the first postmaster of the new town and served as constable for several terms. He built a stable and conducted a livery business for years.

ARDO, SAN

San Ardo is not actually a name, but a shortening of *San Bernardo*. The small oil town in the southern Salinas River Valley region was founded in 1886 on the *Rancho San Bernardo*, granted in 1841 to Mariano and Juan Soberanes. The *Bern* was apparently lopped off later to avoid confusion with San Bernardino. See *Bernardo, Rancho.*

ARGUELLO, POINT

In 1793 Captain George Vancouver sailed past the coastal headland north of Point Concepción in Santa Barbara County and named it for José Darío Argüello (1753-1828), commander of the Monterey presidio. whom the English explorer had met earlier. Later, he commanded the Presidio of Santa Barbara. In 1814, upon the death of the then governor of Alta California, Argüello, as the ranking officer in the province, became acting governor for a year. Thereafter, he became governor of Baja California, serving in that office without compensation for seven years. He died penniless in Guadalajara six years later, at the age of seventy-five. His wife, and mother to his fourteen children, died the following year.

ARMSTRONG REDWOODS STATE NATURAL RESERVE

During the Civil War James Boydston Armstrong (1824-1900) had been commissioned a colonel in the Union Army—a title he would be known by ever after. In 1874 he moved from his native Ohio to Sonoma County, where he went into the lumber business, operating a sawmill north of Guerneville. In 1875 he bought 440 acres of old-growth redwood groves three miles north of Guerneville. Later he gave it to his daughter Kate. It had been his intention for it to be preserved, and eventually operated, as an arboretum. After Kate's death another daughter mounted a campaign to preserve this last remnant of the redwood forest. Her efforts were finally rewarded in 1917 when the County of Sonoma passed an initiative to purchase the property for $80,000. The grove was operated by the county until 1934 when the state took ownership of it. The grove was opened to the public as Armstrong Redwoods State Park in 1936. In 1956 it became a State Natural Reserve. The State Park brochure characterizes its namesake thusly: ". . . mega-logger Colonel James Armstrong, surely one of the few 19th-century timber barons who recognized both the beauty and the board feet in California's redwood groves."

ARNOLD

During the Gold Rush era, the area in Calaveras County around what would be Arnold was comprised of two large ranches where logging was the principal industry. Bob and

Bernice Arnold were the first merchants to settle in the area, arriving in 1933. They bought forty acres from a local lumber company and started the community by building a bar and restaurant and three cabins. When a post office was established a year later, Mrs. Arnold became postmaster.

ARVIN

One of the earliest settlers of the Kern County town was Ralph Haven, the manager of the Home Telephone Co. in San Bernardino, who arrived in 1908 after a two-day horse-and-buggy journey. During the winter he built the first house at the new settlement and planted ten acres of fruit trees. Unfortunately, these projects used up all his cash, so he asked his friend George Richardson and his wife to move into the new house and tend to the orchard while he and his family returned to San Bernardino. The Richardsons and their son, Arvin, lived in the house for a year-and-a-half. When the settlement's well failed, requiring water to be hauled from a canal four miles away, Arvin drilled an irrigation well. He went on to open up its first store and become its postmaster. In gratitude, the town folk named the community after the enterprising young man.

ATHERTON

Faxon D. Atherton (1818-1877) shipped out from his native Massachusetts at the age of eighteen to "seek fame and fortune." And he found it. In Valparaiso, Chile, where he entered the shipping business and married a daughter of one of the country's most distinguished families. Eventually he liquidated his holdings and moved to California, where, in 1860, he bought six-hundred acres of land in Menlo Park in San Mateo County to build an estate, which he would call Valparaiso Park. For the convenience of the owners of the large estates who lived north of Menlo Park, there was a flag stop ("Fair Oaks") on the San Francisco-San Jose Railroad line. In 1923, Menlo Park wished to incorporate its lands to include Fair Oaks. During a meeting of the representatives of the two communities, it became clear to the Fair Oaks property owners that in order to maintain their community as a strictly residential area, they would have to incorporate themselves. Both groups rushed to Sacramento, the Fair Oaks committee arriving first. It was at that time it realized it could not keep the name Fair Oaks—it was the name of a town near Sacramento. So it was decided to honor Atherton who had been one of the first property owners in the south peninsula and name the new town for him.

ATWATER
When, in 1872, the Central Pacific Railroad came through Merced County, a switch was laid next to the warehouse owned by wheat farmer Marshall D. Atwater (1825-1905). It and the building became known as Atwater Switch. When a town was laid out in 1888 by the Merced Land and Fruit Company, it was named for the railroad stop. Atwater had come from Connecticut to California, buying a ranch northwest of Merced that eventually extended over 10,000 acres and which he worked for more than thirty years.

AUSTIN, MOUNT MARY
The mountain summit (elev. 13,052 ft.) in the southern Sierra honors the writer who lived in Inyo County and beautifully described the "long, brown, and lonely land" in such regional classics as *The Land of Little Rain, The Basket Woman,* and *The Ford.* Born and raised in Illinois she came to California with her family when she was twenty. After marrying, she and her husband moved to Lone Pine in the Owens Valley. She remained there, on and off, for twelve years, teaching school and writing. When the valley's water was drained to provide water for Los Angeles, she left Inyo County for good.

AUSTIN CREEK
The Sonoma County waterway is named for Henry Austin, who settled near its mouth in 1856. He is likely the first settler in the county's Ocean township. The creek runs through the **Austin Creek State Recreation Area.**

AVILA BEACH

In 1842, shortly after the secularization of Mission lands by the Mexican government, Don Miguel Ávila (1798-1824) was granted the *Rancho San Miguelito*, 22,136 acres of land along the shoreline of San Luis Obispo Bay and the Valley of the San Luis Obispo River. Ávila had been a Spanish soldier stationed at the Santa Barbara Presidio before becoming a guard at the San Luis Obispo Mission in 1824. Two years later he married into the powerful Pico family, which gave him sufficient influence to gain the land grant. He became the *alcalde* of San Luis Obispo in 1849. In 1867 his son, Miguel, laid out the town of Avila—which later became Avila Beach—and sold parcels to settlers and business proprietors.

B

BAKER

The little Death Valley community started off in 1908 as a station for the now-defunct Tonopah and Tidewater Railroad built a few years earlier by Francis M. "Borax" Smith, primarily to haul borax out of the mines to market. The area was originally known as "Berry," but later renamed "Baker" after Smith's English partner, Richard C. Baker (1858-1937), the company's Mining Director and, later, its president. He is credited with the discovery of the mineral named for him, Bakerite.

BAKER, FORT

It memorializes the English-born Edward Dickinson Baker (1811-1861), a one-time Illinois Congressman for Springfield—he had the distinction of defeating Abraham Lincoln for the office—who moved to San Francisco in 1852 where he practiced law and became active in politics. His acumen with the law and oratory earned him his nickname "The Old Grey Eagle." In 1860 he relocated to Oregon where he was elected to the United States Senate. The following year he volunteered to serve as a Union officer in the Civil War and was mortally wounded in the Battle of Balls Bluff, Virginia. He was the only sitting Senator to be killed in the war. In 1897 the Lime Point Military Reservation in Marin County, which had been established in 1850 to protect the Golden Gate, was renamed Fort Baker in his honor. In 2002 it became part of the Golden Gate National Recreation Area.

Thomas Baker

BAKERSFIELD

The twenty-two year old Thomas Baker (1810-1872) moved to Iowa after studying surveying and law in his native Ohio. There he held a number of offices including that of colonel in the Iowa Territory Militia. When statehood was won, he was elected as a member of the first State Legislature. In 1850 he left for California, settling in Tulare County, where after a few years he was elected to the State Assembly and then to the State Senate. He was instrumental in the passage of the Montgomery Act which offered anyone who reclaimed state swamp and overflow lands a percentage of the recovered land. With this in mind, Baker moved over the Sierra Nevada and south to the Kern Island area in 1857, where he started a large reclamation project that netted him almost 90,000 acres of land. He planted a ten-acre parcel with alfalfa for the use of travelers to feed their animals when journeying from Visalia to Los Angeles and which came to be known as "Baker's field." In 1869 he was appointed to survey a formal township. At the founding ceremony, the residents surprised him by naming it for him. He never lived to see it grow; he died three years later in a typhoid epidemic.

BALBOA ISLAND

This small man-made island situated within Newport Harbor in Orange County is named for the Spanish explorer Vasco Nuñez de Balboa (1475-1515), the first European to see the eastern shore of the Pacific Ocean. He accomplished this after an arduous trek through the jungle of what is now Panama. He claimed the ocean for Spain, opening the way for that country's conquest along the western coast of South America. He did not, however, name the ocean. That was done by Magellan who characterized its waters as calm, *pacifica* in Spanish.

Other Newport sites named for him are **Balboa Beach** and **Balboa Peninsula**. Further south is San Diego's **Balboa Park**, named in 1910 as the result of a contest. **Lake Balboa** is an area in Los Angeles' San Fernando Valley.

BALDWIN PARK

The city in the San Gabriel Valley of Los Angeles County takes its name from the enterprising Elias Jackson "Lucky" Baldwin (1828-1909), the former owner of the *Rancho Puente de San Gabriel*, on which the city is situated. Born in Ohio, he came to California by wagon train in 1853, settling with his family in San Francisco. He earned his nickname by investing early in Comstock silver mining stock and selling at its peak, making a sizable fortune, estimated at $20 million. In 1875 he moved to the San Gabriel Valley, buying up 63,000 agricultural acres. Some of it he subdivided, creating in the process the towns of Arcadia and Monrovia, and building the famous Santa Anita racetrack on his estate.

What is today Baldwin Park was originally called

"Vineland." In 1906 Baldwin decided to establish his own town of "Baldwinville'" nearby. The residents of Vineland opposed the move, feeling that that such competition would threaten the prosperity it had been enjoying, and when legal steps to hinder the project failed, they sought to personally reason with Baldwin, by then almost eighty-years-old. He enjoyed the uproar he had caused. He attended a meeting that had been set up to consider the matter. As he entered the room, he slipped and could have seriously injured himself but for a Vineland resident whose quick action saved him. It was said that this close call turned him away from pursing the idea of Baldwinville. Vineland expressed its gratitude to him by changing its name to Baldwin Park.

BALE GRIST MILL HISTORIC PARK

When HMS *Harriet* ran aground off Monterey in 1837, one of the few survivors was the ship's surgeon, Dr Edward Turner Bale (1811-1849). Sailing from his native Ireland, it turned out to be propitious that he landed in Monterey; at that time its leading physician had fallen into disfavor for his part in a failed attempt to overthrow the Governor. Though Bale had a reputation for drinking and quarreling--he was twice jailed, once for bootlegging, the other time for shooting at the brother of General Mariano Vallejo--he became a successful doctor, converted to Catholicism, married Vallejo's niece and became a Mexican citizen. He was granted the 18,000-acre *Rancho Carne Humana*, which comprised the land between present-day Rutherford and Calistoga in the Napa Valley, and where he made his home with his wife and six children. In 1846 he built a water-powered grist mill on the land that was eventually (in 1974) granted to the state and is now part of the Bale Grist Mill Historic Park. With news of the discovery of gold in 1848 he headed "for the hills," but contracted a fatal fever and died the following year. One of Bale's daughters married Charles Krug who planted grapes on land just north of St. Helena, land which had been her dowry.

BANNING

22

The Riverside County city is named for Phineas Banning (1830-1895), known as the "Father of the Port of Los Angeles." Born in Wilmington, Delaware, at thirteen he left home with only a fifty-cent piece in his pocket to work in Philadelphia. When he was twenty he signed up to work his way to California on a ship. He arrived at San Pedro, then a small fishing village, where he became a stagecoach driver on the line that connected it to Los Angeles, twenty miles inland. An ambitious young man, he soon started his own stage line which in time earned him a small fortune.

Banning used his stagecoach profits to buy, with a group of other local investors, 640 acres of land next to San Pedro for the expansion of the port. It was soon incorporated as "Wilmington," after Banning's home town.

During the Civil War, Banning, a fervent abolitionist, sold land to the Union at a nominal price, for which the government gave him the honorary title of brigadier general of the California First Brigade of the National Guard. Although it was purely symbolic, he insisted on being referred to as "General Banning" the last twenty years of his life, during which time he became a key figure in regional business enterprises, politics, and society, and served as a State Senator from 1865 to 1868. Ironically, Banning died while on a business trip to San Francisco, after being run over by an express wagon. California historian Kevin Starr said of Banning that he "perhaps embodies this first phase of economic entrepreneurship in Southern California, with its diversity and optimism, its unambiguous satisfaction in fulfilling obvious and necessary needs."

The Riverside County city of Banning was originally known as Moore City. When a local church needed funds to build a rectory, Banning offered the money if the city would be named for him. A deal was struck and the name was changed. He never lived there.

BARBARA, SANTA

The coastal city, county, channel, and island are named for the fourth-century saint Barbara. In 1602 Vizcaíno bestowed it in gratitude for having survived a storm in the Channel on December 3, the eve of her feast day. Barbara was the daughter of a rich pagan who locked her in a tower to keep her from the outside world. Before starting a journey he ordered that a bath house for her be erected. While he was gone Barbara had three windows put in it, as a symbol of the Trinity. When her father returned, she told him that she was a Christian.. He was so incensed, he dragged her before the prefect of the province who had her tortured and then condemned to death by beheading, which was carried out by the father himself.

BARDSDALE

The Ventura County community was founded in 1889 on the *Rancho Sespe* land grant by a developer who had bought the land from Thomas R. Bard (1841-1915) and who named it in the latter's honor. Bard, a Pennsylvanian and Civil War veteran, moved to the county in 1864, where he became a member of the Board of Supervisors (1868-1873), laid out the town of Port Hueneme, and served on the State Board of Agriculture (1886-1887). In 1899 he was elected to the U. S. Senate and served from 1900 to 1905. He was defeated for re-election and spent his last years managing his businesses.

BARSTOW

Located in San Bernardino County, the desert city was founded in 1880 during a silver-mining rush. In 1886 it was named to honor William Barstow Strong (1837-1914), at that time the president of the Atchison, Topeka and Santa Fe Railway which maintained construction and repair facilities there. During his tenure (1881-1889), he developed the Santa Fe into a major transcontinental railroad with the expansion of more than 7,000 miles of right-of-way. The town fathers wanted to name it Strong, but as a town by that name (also named after the railroad executive) already existed in Kansas, they had to settle for his middle name.

BEALE AIR FORCE BASE

The base--near Marysville in Yuba County--is named for Brigadier General Edward Fitzgerald Beale (1822-1893). He graduated from the Naval Academy, served in the California State Militia, led the experiment to replace Army mules with camels, and, as owner of about 200,000 acres (*Rancho Tejon*), was one of California's largest landholders. Space prevents a full survey of his remarkable career: here is how one encyclopedia summed it up: "He was naval officer, military general, explorer, frontiersman, Indian affairs superintendent, California rancher, diplomat, and friend of Kit Carson, Buffalo Bill Cody and Ulysses S. Grant." Camp Beale opened in October 1942 as a training site for the 13th Armored and the 81st and 96th Infantry Divisions. During World War II, its 86,000 acres were home for more than 60,000 soldiers, a prisoner-of-war encampment and a 1000-bed hospital. In 1948 the camp was transferred from the Army to the Air Force. The **Beale Mountains** in the Mojave National Preserve are named for the general as well.

Jim Beckwourth

BECKWOURTH PASS

The discovery of the northern Sierra Nevada pass in eastern Plumas County opened the pioneer route to the Sacramento Valley. It was named for James ("Jim") P.

Beckwourth (1798-1867), a key figure in the exploration of the West. Although there were people of various races and nationalities on the early frontier, Beckwourth was the only African-American who wrote down his life story, ranging from adventures in the Florida everglades to the Pacific Ocean and from Canada to Mexico. His memoirs were dictated in 1854 and 1855 to Thomas D. Bonner, an itinerant Justice of the Peace in California's gold fields. After some "polishing up" by Bonner, his robust narrative, *The Life and Adventures of James P. Beckwourth, Mountaineer, Scout, and Pioneer, and Chief of the Crow Nation of Indians* was published by Harper and Row in 1856.

He was one of thirteen children born in Virginia to an Irish-American plantation owner and an African-American slave. The family moved to Missouri where he was emancipated and educated by his father. He was not only literate, but also fluent in French, Spanish, and several Native American dialects. After working in New Orleans as a roustabout, he headed west to the Rocky Mountains where he became a trapper and, within a few years, a "mountain man." In 1828 he was adopted into a Crow Indian tribe whose chief believed him his long-lost son who had been captured when a child by the Cheyenne. For the next half-dozen years he lived and fought as an Indian, before hitting the trail for the Southwest. During the Gold Rush, he headed to California.

The Beckwourth Pass came out of the California Trail, a system of wagon roads and pack trails used since 1841 by California-bound emigrants. Discovered by Beckwourth around 1850, it branched off the main road at Truckee Meadows and ended at Bidwell's Bar, a mining camp now under the waters of Lake Oroville. He came upon it while searching for a "Gold Lake" reputed to be in northern California. He set out to raise money to build a road through the pass to American Valley, which was successful, and opened up to wagons in 1851. The following year Beckwourth established a trading post, "War Horse Ranch," in the Sierra Valley but after a few years traffic on his road diminished as other roads were developed. In 1866, while working in Fort Laramie,

Wyoming, he died on a hunting trip with his adopted people, the Crow Indians.

The State's first poet laureate, Ina Coolbrith, who as an eleven-year-old came through the Pass with her parents, escorted by Jim Beckwourth, remembered him as "one of the most beautiful creatures that ever lived. He was rather dark and wore his hair in two long braids, twisted with colored cord that gave him a picturesque appearance. He wore a leather coat and moccasins and rode a horse without a saddle." In 1994 the Postal Service issued a commemorative stamp with a portrait of Beckwourth as part of a series of "Legends of the West."

BELL

For most of the nineteenth century, the land that now encompasses the city of Bell in Los Angeles County was part of the 30,000-acre *Rancho San Antonio*. When a land boom hit the area between 1870 and 1890, most of it was subdivided into small holdings which were acquired by arriving settlers. James George Bell (1831-1911) bought about 360 acres of it—which he dubbed "Bell Station Ranch"—and helped in its development as a small farming and cattle-raising community known as Obed. In 1898 it changed its name to honor Bell. His son Alphonzo Bell developed Westwood, Beverly Hills, Pacific Palisades and Bel-Air. The adjacent **Bell Gardens**, incorporated in 1971, was named after its neighbor.

BELL CANYON

The gated residential Ventura County community is located in the Simi Hills. Up to 1967 it was a cattle ranch. When an equestrian center was built, developers purchased what was to be Bell Canyon, and built the Woodland Hills Country Estates which quickly sold 800 home sites. The new owners renamed the community "Bell Canyon,' after Charles A. Bell (1863-1917) the original homesteader there, and a lawyer who was Justice of the Peace of Calabasas in 1906 and was rumored to have lost his right arm in a gun battle while raiding a moonshiner in 1887.

BENBOW LAKE
The "Hotel Benbow" in Garberville, Humboldt County, opened to the public in 1926. Built by the nine children of Arthur Benbow, it became a popular destination for tourists traveling up the newly completed Redwood Highway. In order to provide power for the new development in the valley, a concrete dam was constructed across the south fork of the Eel River in 1928. The dam not only provided power but also created Benbow Lake. The Benbow family, interested in preserving the natural scene around the hotel and along the river, made efforts to place the land under State protection. In 1956 funds were approved and it became the **Benbow Lake State Recreation Area.**

BENECIA
The Solano County city was the first community in California to be founded by Anglo Americans, unlike those that arose from the earlier Spanish missions, forts and trading posts. It was established in 1847 on land purchased for a hundred dollars from General Mariano C. Vallejo, the last Mexican Commandant-General in California. It served as the state capital for thirteen months during 1853 and 1854 and was named in honor of the General's wife, Doña Francisca Benicia Carrillo de Vallejo (1816-18??). Initially the town was to be named "Francisca," but had to be changed to her second name when the leaders on the new city of Yerba Buena succeeded in obtaining the official designation of "San Francisco." After the city's founding, she began to go by the name of Doña Benicia instead of Francisca. She was the mother of sixteen children of which ten survived to adulthood.

BENITO COUNTY, SAN
"Benito" is the Spanish name for the Italian Saint Benedict (c.480-c.543), founder of the Benedictine Order, considered the father of western monasticism. The county took its name from the **San Benito Valley**, so christened because it was "discovered" by Gaspar de Portolá on that saint's feast day.

28

BENSON LAKE

Colonel Harry C. Benson (1857-1924) was commissioned in the Army in 1882 upon graduating from West Point. He first served with the artillery, but finding it dull, transferred to the cavalry where he became involved in the campaign to capture Geronimo. In 1887 he returned to West Point as mathematics instructor for a few years before being sent to the Presidio of San Francisco where he was able to participate in the annual duty assignments at Yosemite and had the distinction, in 1895, of having both Benson Lake and **Benson Pass** named for him. During the Spanish-American War he acted as the collector of customs in Cuba and, later, in the Philippines. In 1905 he served as Superintendent of Yosemite, a post he held for three years before being transferred to superintend Yellowstone National Park. In 1911 he was assigned to the position of Chief of Staff of the Philippines Department, where he remained until his retirement four years later.

George Berkeley

BERKELEY

The home of the University of California came to its name after long discussion by its first trustees in 1866, the year of its founding. They decided to honor the Irish

29

philosopher George Berkeley (1685-1753), Bishop of Cloyne, because of a poem he wrote promoting education in America. When he had been appointed Dean of Derry in 1724 he hoped to realize his ambition to found a college in the New World, believing that Europe was on the decline and the only hope for the future of civilization lay in the British colonies in America. The spirit of the endeavor is embodied in his poem "America or The Muse's Refuge: A Prophecy," which moved the California trustees to their action and included the verse: "Westward the course of empire takes its way/The four first acts already past,/A fifth shall close the drama with the day; / Time's noblest offspring is the last."

In 1898 "Berkeley," as the settled area round the campus was known, merged with the adjacent community of Oceanview and they incorporated officially as the city of Berkeley.

BERNAL HEIGHTS

The San Francisco neighborhood was originally part of the 4,446-acre *Rancho Rincón de las Salinas y Potrero Nuevo* granted in 1839 to José Cornelio de Bernal (1796-1842), a grandson of a soldier in Anza's 1776 expedition.

BERNARDINO, SAN

The name was supposedly given in 1810 by the Franciscan Francisco Dumatz, of the San Gabriel Mission, who led his company into an undiscovered valley. In observance of the Feast day of St. Bernardine of Siena (1380-1444), he named it for the saint. It was later given to the nearby mountain range and then the city and county. The Franciscan saint, often called the "Apostle of Italy," is accounted to have been the greatest preacher of his day, sermonizing throughout Italy.

BERNARDO, RANCHO SAN

The northern San Diego County community began as an 18,000-acre Spanish land grant in 1763 known as *La Cañada de San Bernardo* ("The Gorge of St. Bernard.") It is thought to be named for Saint Bernard of Clairvaux (1090-

1153), the French monk who led the Second Crusade.

BERRYESSA, LAKE

Nasario Antonio Berryessa served as a corporal at the San Francisco Presidio from 1819 to 1824, after which he moved to what is now Napa County. He brought with him about a hundred Pomo Indians to help with raising stock. Over time he would own herds of 5,000 cattle and 20,000 horses. His sons José de Jesus (1814-1866) and Sisto Antonio (1818-1847) moved to the ranch and, in 1842. petitioned the governor for the land known as *El Rancho de las Putas*. It was granted the following year and at almost 36,000 acres was one of the largest grants in California history. Unfortunately, the brothers were gamblers and in 1860 were unable to make due on a $1645 gambling debt and were forced to sell their remaining 26,000 acres in a county auction for $2,000. The buyer turned around and sold it for a $100.000 to a "land company" which subdivided it into farm properties, leaving room for the development of the town of Monticello in 1870. The Monticello Dam was constructed in order to provide irrigation for area residents. The reservoir formed behind the dam was christened Lake Berryessa in 1957 to honor the original settlers.

John &Annie Bidwell

BIDWELL PARK

In 1905 Annie Bidwell, the widow of General John Bidwell (1819-1900), donated 2500 acres of land in Chico to be used as a city park. The General was a man of parts. He led the first overland expedition to California in 1841, a six-month trek of immense difficulty. Upon his arrival, he went to work for John A. Sutter and became a Mexican citizen. Though he discovered gold on the Feather River in 1848, his interests turned to farming. He bought a 22,000-acre ranch in Chico, where he remained the rest of his life. Even though he had been commissioned as a general in the state militia, he was more interested in politics than the military. In 1865 he was elected to Congress and ran (unsuccessfully) for governor three times, and was the Prohibition Party's nominee for President in 1892. His home is now the **Bidwell Mansion State Historic Park**. **Bidwell-Sacramento River State Park** in Butte County, a lake in Lassen County, a fort and a peak in Modoc County, and a point in the Mendocino National Forest are all named for him as well.

BIGGS

Located in the southwest portion of Butte County, it was founded in 1871 as "Biggs Station" by the California and Oregon Railroad for Major Marion Biggs (1823-1910), a local civic leader who had a ranch there. He hailed from Missouri where he was a county sheriff for four years, before moving permanently to California in 1864. There he was a cattle buyer and politician, serving two terms in the State Assembly (from Butte and Sacramento Counties, respectively) before being elected in 1887 as a Democrat to the U. S. House of Representatives. He made his home in Gridley, where he lived until his death.

BISHOP

The eastern High Sierra community in Inyo County is named for one of the first white settlers in the area, Samuel Addison Bishop (1786-1864). Originally from Virginia, he left for the California gold fields in 1849, becoming, in turn, an Indian fighter, cattleman, and businessman,. The

32

city which bears his name came into being due to the need for beef in a booming mining camp some eighty miles to the north, Aurora, Nevada. (Aurora was then thought to be on the western side of the border and was the county seat of Mono County, California). At the time cattle ranchers drove their herds some three hundred miles from the San Joaquin Valley through the southern Sierra at Walker Pass, up the Owens Valley, and then through Adobe Meadows to Aurora. Along the way some of them noticed that the unsettled northern Owens Valley was ideal for raising livestock. To avoid the long journey from the other side of the mountains, a few decided to settle there. Driving some six hundred head of cattle and fifty horses, Bishop, his wife and several hired hands arrived in the valley in 1861 from Fort Tejon in the Tehachapi Mountains in Kern County. Establishing a homestead, the San Francis Ranch, along the creek which still bears his name, Bishop set up a market to sell beef to the miners and business owners in Aurora. By the following year, a frontier settlement known as Bishop Creek was established a few miles east of Bishop's ranch. He and his family returned to Fort Tejon a few years later—where he would serve as a county supervisor--but the small settlement continued to prosper. In 1889, it dropped "Creek" from its name and became known simply as Bishop.

BLISS STATE PARK, D. L.

The park on Lake Tahoe's west shore is named for lumberman, railroad owner, and banker of the region, Duane Leroy Bliss (1833-1907), who was instrumental in the early efforts to increase tourism in Lake Tahoe. In 1893 he founded the Lake Tahoe Transportation Company to build a rail line to carry visitors to the lake. Bliss had left his home in Massachusetts when he was sixteen to seek gold in California where he worked a small claim near Marysville, before moving to Nevada where he became a partner in a banking firm. He built a summer home at Tahoe in 1872, where he formed a successful logging company. In 1929 his family donated almost a thousand acres to the State Park system.

BLYTHE

In 1908 the Palo Verde Land and Water Company named the Riverside County town in honor of San Francisco millionaire Thomas H. Blythe (1822-1883). He was an obscure Englishman, whose real name was Thomas H. Williams, who came to California in 1849, and began buying real estate in the center of San Francisco and elsewhere which was valued at over $3 million at his death. He used some of his fortune to purchase about 40,000 acres of the Palo Verde Valley (near the center of what is now the city of Blythe) from the State under the Swamp and Overflow Act of 1868 which gave land that was a perennial swamp or subject to flooding to anyone who would fill, drain, or put the land to good use. In 1879 he began working on irrigation projects to bring water from the Colorado River to the land. He died of a heart attack before the work could be completed. His creditors quickly froze his assets so that money for the Palo Verde Valley was cut off. As Blythe was unmarried and left no will, his estate was tied up in court for ten years until it was finally settled by the U. S. Supreme Court. There was no further agricultural development in the valley until 1908 when the Laguna Dam was built above Yuma. Palo Verde then changed its name to honor Blythe.

BODEGA BAY

Lt. Juan Francisco de la Bodega y Quadra (1743-1794), a Peruvian sailing for Spain and part of a naval expedition exploring the western coast of North America, is credited with discovering, in 1775, the Sonoma County bay which bears his name.

BODIE

This gold-mining ghost town in Mono County once had a population of over ten thousand. It was named for a '49er originally from Poughkeepsie, New York named Waterman "William" S. Body (1814-1859) also known as William S. Bodey, who had panned for gold in the hills north of Mono Lake in 1859 and built a cabin about four miles from the site of the present town. The following year he froze to death in a snowstorm. A friend helped to establish a mining camp, which took on Body's name. The change in the spelling of the town, often attributed to an illiterate sign painter, was actually a deliberate attempt to make sure it was pronounced correctly. In 1877 the Standard Company found gold thereabouts and a rush ensued, transforming Bodie from a hamlet of about twenty people to a boomtown. Designated as a National Historic Site and a **State Historic Park** in 1962, the remains of Bodie are being preserved in a state of "arrested decay." It is now listed as one of the world's one hundred most endangered sites by the World Monuments Watch. The **Bodie Hills** are nearby.

BOGGS MOUNTAIN

It is named for Henry C. Boggs (1820-1898), a Lake County pioneer who once owned most of the area now known as **Boggs Mountain Demonstration State Forest**. He was the son of a Napa Valley farmer, merchant and former governor of the state of Missouri. In 1880 he bought several thousand acres of mountain-top south of Clear Lake and just north of the headwaters of Putah Creek, moved his sawmill there and cut stands of timber. The Farmers Savings Bank of Lakeport, of which Boggs was president, became the owners of the property in 1898. Around 1950 the California Department of Forestry made it a demonstration forest, an experiment in restoration and sustainable forestry, at which time all the timber interests and titles were conveyed to the state.

BOONVILLE

Soon after Walter Anderson returned in the 1850s to settle in the Mendocino County valley named for him, the first town was founded, called "The Corners." Soon afterwards, Alonzo Kendall constructed a hotel, and stores followed and a little community known as Kendall's City soon took root. In 1858 W. W. Boone (a distant relative of Daniel Boone) settled in Anderson Valley and took over Kendall's store and renamed the town for himself—Booneville.

35

Later the "e" was dropped and it became Boonville.

BOTHE-NAPA VALLEY STATE PARK

Located on Ritchey Creek in Napa Valley, it is named for Reinhold Bothe who, in 1929, bought part of the estate previously owned by Lillie Hitchcock Coit, an eccentric enamored of fire fighting (think Coit Tower in San Francisco). He and his wife turned it into a private resort known as Paradise Park, replete with cabins, lodge, swimming pool, and an airstrip. It was popular during the 1930s, less so after World War II. The state park system purchased it from Bothe in 1960.

BOYES HOT SPRINGS

An English couple, Captain Henry E. Boyes (1844-1919) and his wife, were in Sonoma Valley in the 1880s in search of a healthy climate for the latter. They had heard of springs on the property of a San Francisco physician named T. M. Leavenworth that was supposed to have restorative benefits. The doctor had built a small bathhouse and a tank of the site. The "health resort" folded and in 1888 the Boyeses bought the land. In 1895, while drilling a well, they struck 112-degree water. Within five years they completed construction of the Boyes Hot Springs Resort Hotel which, in one form or another, and under different ownership, has continued to this day. The surrounding community retains the name of the original hot springs.

BOYLE HEIGHTS

This Los Angeles eastside neighborhood is named for Andrew Boyle (1818-1871), an Irishman who immigrated to the United States when he was fourteen. He came to the area in 1858 after living in San Francisco, purchased pasture and vineyard land at twenty-five cents an acre, and constructed the first brick residence east of the Los Angeles River. An entrepreneur, he established a wine-growing concern, operated a shoe store, and served on the City Council.

BRADBURY

Less than two square miles in area, the secluded city, twenty miles from downtown Los Angeles, just may have more horses than citizens. It has no stores, gas stations, apartment buildings, or traffic lights. It was named for Lewis Leon Bradbury, Sr. (1823-1892), originally of Bangor, Maine, who came west to Oregon where he started a dry goods business. In the early 1860s he went to Mexico where he developed the rich Tajo mine, in which he owned the controlling interest and where he made a fortune. About 1880 he and his family relocated to Oakland and then to southern California, where he began to invest in real estate. In 1883 he acquired 2750 acres of the *Rancho Azusa de Duarte* and built an estate that would become the city of Bradbury, incorporated in 1957. He built the landmark Bradbury building in downtown Los Angeles, but died before its completion in 1893.

BRADLEY

The Monterey County community was named for, and sprung from, land owned by Bradley Varnum Sargent (1828-1893) at the time the Southern Pacific line reached it in 1886. Sargent had come to California from New Hampshire in 1849 with his three brothers. He moved to Monterey County in 1857 and bought *Rancho Potrero de San Carlos* in Carmel Valley and *Rancho San Francisquito*, as well as *Rancho La Pestilencia*, so-called because of the stench of sulfur springs on the land, and where the town of Bradley was situated. He served several times as a County Supervisor and a term in the State Senate in 1886.

BRAGG, FORT

Founded in 1885, the Mendocino County town is named for an Army post founded on the site thirty years earlier that honored West Point graduate and North Carolinian Braxton Bragg (1817-1876), a Lieutenant Colonel in the Mexican War. Unfortunately, his Civil War career was not so distinguished. As a Confederate general, he was routed at Chattanooga and removed from command. After the war he served as Alabama's chief engineer and then settled in Galveston, Texas, where he remained until his death.

BRANCIFORTE CREEK

San Lorenzo River's largest tributary takes its name from the *Villa de Branciforte*, founded in 1796, the last Spanish colonial town to be established in California. It was named for the Viceroy of New Spain serving at the time of its founding, Don Miguel de la Grua Talamanca Branciforte, Marques de Branciforte (1755-1812), a man characterized by one historian as "uncaring, incompetent, and utterly corrupt."

Samuel Brannan

BRANNAN ISLAND

At the gateway to the Sacramento-San Joaquin Delta, the island was named for Samuel Brannan (1819-1889), at one time the wealthiest man in California. Born in Maine, he became a Mormon and led a group of his co-religionists to San Francisco in 1846. There he became an ambitious leader. He constructed flourmills, bought land, and printed the *California Star*, San Francisco's first newspaper. In the fall of 1847 he opened a store at Sutter's Fort. A few months later, there were rumors that gold had been found nearby at Coloma. In early May, Brannan headed to the mines to check it out. He learned "there was more gold than all the people in California could take out in fifty years." He made plans for a second store, then packed.

some of the gold and returned to San Francisco where he showed it off, shouting "Gold! Gold! Gold! Gold from the American River!" By the middle of June, three-quarters of the male population had left town for the mines.

Brannan did not prospect for gold himself, rather the precious metal made his stores fantastic profits by selling as much as $5,000 (about $125,000 in today's dollars) in goods per day to miners. He opened a third store. He owned property in San Francisco and was the largest landowner in the new town of Sacramento. He made money with energy and recklessness., but also exhibited such destructive impulses as fighting, adultery, and drinking. With property to defend, Brannan took up a vigilante brand of law and order and would play a key role in San Francisco's Vigilance Committee.

During the 1850s and 1860s Brannan was known as the richest man in the State. The chaos of the Gold Rush had played to his business instincts, but he dived into some projects like a gambler. He once sailed to Hawaii to overthrow the king, a coup that failed. He bought 3,000 acres in Napa Valley, hired Japanese gardeners to tend the land and bought 800 horses. He called his new resort Calistoga and catered to San Francisco's wealthy. In typical fashion, Brannan got in a drunken fight one night with some employees. He was shot eight times. but survived.

Bitter about her husband's notorious infidelity, Brannan's wife filed for divorce and demanded a cash settlement. Brannan was forced to transform his huge paper fortune into cash in 1870 when the California economy was at a low point. His empire collapsed. He spent the next two decades negotiating land deals in Mexico, but his schemes failed. Broke, he moved to Nogales, Arizona. In 1887 Brannan sold pencils door-to-door to raise the money for a trip to San Francisco. The newspapers covered the former tycoon's visit. One reporter described him as "old, gray, broken in strength, able only to get about with the aid of a cane. The old keenness of the eye alone shows that his spirit has survived the decay of his body." Brannan died on small fruit farm outside San Diego on 1889, leaving his children but a few dollars apiece.

In the 1950s the island became a state park, **Brannan Island State Recreation Area.**

BRAWLEY

The Imperial County city was conceived by the Imperial Land Company in 1902 and was to be called Braly for J. H. Braly, a Los Angeles banker who had underwritten 4000 shares of stock (representing a like number of acres of land) of the company with the intention of developing a town site. Soon after, a circular released by the federal government was published which claimed that nothing would grow in the desert area, even with an unlimited source of water. Though not true, Braly believed it and asked the Imperial Land Company to be released from his contract. It told him that it expected to build a city on the land and call it Braly, but J. H. wanted nothing to do with the Imperial Valley, nor did he want his name connected with what he clearly saw as a failure. Eventually the Company bought back his shares. One of its principals had a friend in Chicago by the name of Brawley and suggested, as a compromise, the town be called by that name.

BREWER, MOUNT

William H. Brewer (1828-1910) assisted Josiah Whitney on his geological survey of California during the 1860s. Survey members named Mt. Brewer in Kings Canyon National Park for him after he made the first ascent in 1864. He was the chief of the field party that explored the central High Sierra in the same year. His journals were published as *Up and Down California* in 1930. After his California ventures, he returned to the East where he was a professor of agriculture at Yale for forty years.

BRISBANE

The name was selected by Arthur Annis (1881-1970), the man who developed the town south of San Francisco in San Mateo County. He came to what was then called Visitacion City in 1929 and by his promotion of affordable housing grew the population tenfold in five years. To

40

avoid confusion with the San Francisco district of Visitacion Valley, he proposed that the city change its name to Brisbane. Why Brisbane? According to Annis's daughter, he named it after the city in Australia. Others believed that he named it in honor of a then popular newspaper editor named Arthur Brisbane (1864-1936), who was the owner of a palatial home in the city. Both theories have their supporters; in either event the name is still eponymous as the Australian city is named after a Governor of New South Wales of the 1820s, Sir Thomas Brisbane (1773-1860).

David C. Broderick

BRODERICK, MOUNT

"Broderick" was the original name given to the tall granite dome of Yosemite named Liberty Cap by the Whitney Survey in 1865. The name was transferred later to what is today called Mt. Broderick hard by the taller dome. Its namesake is David C. Broderick (1820-1859), the Irish-born U. S. Senator from California (1857-1859), probably best remembered for his participation in the last formal duel fought in California. While in the Senate he voted against the expansion of slavery despite Southern sympathizers in the California legislature. The pro-slavery California Supreme Court justice David Terry, blamed

Broderick for his defeat for re-election to the bench in 1859. Broderick was overheard by a friend of Terry's saying: "I have said that I considered him the only honest man on the supreme bench, but I now take it all back." This was the provocation that led Terry to "demand satisfaction." The duel was fought, and Broderick mortally wounded. On his deathbed, he said: "They killed me because I was opposed to the extension of slavery and the corruption of justice." Terry was tried and acquitted in Marin County. The duel resulted in post-mortem martyrdom for Broderick, and aroused such a hatred for Terry in San Francisco that he was forced to retire to Stockton.

BRUNO, SAN
Captain Bruno de Heceta (1744-1807) explored the western shore of the San Francisco Bay in 1775. He named the largest land mass on that side of the peninsula **Mount San Bruno**, after his patron saint, Saint Bruno the Confessor (1033-1101). Born in Cologne, Germany, St. Bruno was a teacher, writer, monk and founder of the Carthusian order of monks. The City of San Bruno was named after the mountain, which is now part of **San Bruno Mountain State Park**.

BUELLTON
The roots of the town on Highway 101 in northern Santa Barbara County can be traced to Rufus Thompson ("R.T.") Buell (1827-1905). He grew up on a farm in Vermont before attending Oberlin College in Ohio. In 1853 the reports of the discovery of gold in California convinced him to try his luck there. He boarded the *Yankee Blade* in New York for the trip around Cape Horn to San Francisco. After a hundred days of ocean travel the steamer made port and with fifty-four cents in his pocket Buell headed for the gold fields at Bidwell's Bar. A year later he started a successful dairy farm at Point Reyes in Marin County, which he ran for eight years. He then bought land in the Santa Ynez Valley, the 26,000-acre *Rancho San Carlos de Jonata* and the *Rancho El Capitan*. He

built a successful horse and cattle ranch and dairy farm and by 1875 operated Buell Ranch as a town, complete with a general store, a post office, bunkhouses, blacksmith shop and family homes.

BUNNELL POINT

The point of land in Yosemite honors Lafayette Houghton Bunnell (1824-1903). Born at Rochester, New York, he became interested in the local Indians, learning several of their languages. After serving in the Army during the Mexican War, he came to California in 1849 where he joined the Mariposa Battalion, organized to suppress Indian raids and which, in 1851, was the first party of white men to enter Yosemite Valley. It was Bunnell who proposed the name *Yosemite* for the valley. He returned there on a second expedition and remained in California, trading, mining, and surveying, for five or six years before returning to the East. In 1861 he re-enlisted in the Army and served throughout the Civil War. In his retirement he published *Discovery of the Yosemite* (1880).

BURBANK

The city in Los Angeles County is not named for Luther Burbank, the famous horticulturist, as many believe. Rather, it is named for a Los Angeles dentist named David Burbank (1821-1895). Born in New Hampshire, he traveled by covered wagon to California in the 1850s, setting up a dental practice first in San Francisco, then Los Angeles. He had been active in local real estate when, in 1867, he bought about 10,000 acres of two Spanish land grants, *Rancho San Rafael* and *Rancho La Providencia.*, where he raised sheep, built a house (on what would later be the Warner Brother backlot) and sold off small plots. Realizing that bringing in the railroad would increase the property's value, he sold to the Southern Pacific a stretch of right-of-way for a dollar. During the rate war between it and the Santa Fe, low fares brought streams of people to California and Burbank seized the opportunity. In 1886 he sold 9000 acres of property to a group of land speculators for $250,000 and Providencia Land, Water and Development

Co. was formed. It laid out a business district and divided surrounding properties into small farms and residential lots. It called the town Burbank and opened the tract for sale on May 1, 1887.

Anson Burlingame

BURLINGAME

This toney residential community south of San Francisco is named for a man who never lived there, Anson Burlingame (1820-1870), who Lincoln appointed as Minister to China in 1861. He was a Harvard Law School graduate, a senator in the Massachusetts legislature, and member of the U.S. House of Representatives before accepting the ambassadorship. On a visit in 1868 to see the then-landowner William C. Ralston, founder of the Bank of California, Burlingame was so impressed by the lush landscape that he chose 1100 acres to use after he retired. In his honor Ralston named the new town site after him. Unfortunately, he did not have the opportunity to retire there, having died two years later while on a diplomatic mission to Russia.

BURNEY

The Shasta County town was named after Samuel Burney, a drifter from South Carolina who arrived in the area in the autumn of 1858. A few months later he was acting as caretaker for the property of a neighbor, whose ill-treatment of Native American women angered their people. A group of them came seeking revenge, and the luckless Burney paid for his neighbor's action with his life. Over time Burney's name was given to the town as well as a mountain, creek and falls, the last becoming the centerpiece of **McArthur Burney Falls Memorial State Park**. The sons of early settlers John and Catherine McArthur, afraid that the falls would be destroyed by power companies, bought 160 acres surrounding the falls and in 1920 deeded the property to the State Board of Forestry, requesting only that it be named for their parents.

BURTON CREEK STATE PARK

The Lake Tahoe park is named after Homer D. Burton, who listed his occupation as farmer, and occupied a half section of property (320 acres) near Lake Forest in 1858 or 1859. Burton cut timothy hay for the freighting trade, and raised garden vegetables, buck-wheat, and oats. By 1871, he added a lake front resort to his holdings and named it "Burton's Island Farm and Hotel." **Burton Creek** still bears his name. In 1884 he sold the property to a dairy farmer. Over the next ninety years the property was operated as a dairy farm and logging company by various interests until it was acquired by California State Parks in 1977.

C

Juan Rodriguez Cabrillo

CABRILLO NATIONAL MONUMENT
The Portuguese explorer Joao Rodrigues Cabrilho (c.

1499- 1543)--better known under the Spanish version of his name, Juan Rodríguez Cabrillo—is credited with the European discovery of what is now California. Prior to his California expedition, he had already joined some voyages of discovery. He had come to New Spain (Mexico) with Panfilo de Narvaez to oppose Hernan Cortés, shifted alliance to Cortés, helped the founding of the city of Oaxaca, joined Pedro de Alvarado in his central American conquests, and had become rich from mining gold in Guatemala. In 1542 Antonio de Mendoza, the viceroy of New Spain, asked him to explore the northern limits of its Pacific coast. Cabrillo departed Navidad (present-day Acapulco) on June 27, 1542, and sailed north to Baja California. He went further along the coast, and discovered San Diego Bay and Santa Barbara. Although he reached the Russian River, he missed Monterey Bay and San Francisco Bay. Looking for a place to spend the winter, he made land on San Miguel Island in the Santa Barbara Channel. There he got into a fight with Indians, and died of the complications of a broken leg. In his day the Cabrillo expedition had no major impact; Spain did not make anything of its claims to California until the late eighteenth century when colonization began.

Cabrillo National Monument, established by order of President Woodrow Wilson in 1913, sits at the discoverer's landing place in San Diego. A **Cabrillo Point** in both Mendocino and Monterey counties is named for him as well.

CADY MOUNTAINS

The name of the San Bernardino mountain range retains the memory of Camp Cady, a nineteenth century military post about twenty miles east of Barstow in San Bernardino County. Erected in 1860, it was named for Major Albemarle Cady (1809-1865) of the Sixth Infantry, then in command of Fort Yuma. It served as the base for a series of camps, redoubts, and forts along the Old Government Road to Fort Mojave and the Salt Lake Road, with campaigns waged against the Paiutes and Shoshones. It was abandoned in 1871.

Cady, a West Point graduate, saw duty fighting Indians in Florida and fought in the Mexican War. At the beginning of the Civil War he was on duty on the Pacific coast, and remained there until his retirement in 1864, at which time he received the brevet of brigadier-general.

CALPELLA

This area in Mendocino County's Ukiah Valley was named in the 1850s after Kalpela, chief of a local Northern Pomo village. The name was subsequently applied to his people by the settlers, and then to the area.

CAMARILLO

The Ventura County city was once part of the original 10,000-acre *Rancho Calleguas*, one of the last of the Mexican land grants. It was originally conveyed to José Pedro Ruíz by Governor Alvarado in 1847. In 1875 it passed to Juan Camarillo (1812-1880), a veteran of the 1834 Hijar-Padres Expedition into what was then largely unsettled Alta California. Significant to the location of the town was the Southern Pacific Railroad's decision to lay tracks through the area in 1898. Overriding the objections of the modest sons of Juan Camarillo, railroad officials named the town "Camarillo" in 1899.

CAMERON PARK

The El Dorado County community is named for former champion rodeo-rider Robert "Larry" Cameron (1904-1992). He made a fortune as an automobile dealer in North Sacramento—his dealership was at one time the largest in the world. He sold out in 1962 and used his profits to buy 5,000 acres in the scenic foothills for ranching. In the ensuing years, with the help of other investors, he slowly divided the "Cameron Estates" into lots of varying sizes for resale as residences. He disposed of most of his holdings in 1965 and moved to Rescue.

CAMPBELL

Benjamin Campbell (1826-1907) headed west from his Kentucky home in 1846 with his family, having traveled on

48

the first part of the overland journey with the Donner party, settling in Santa Clara County. When he was twenty-five he claimed 160 acres of land as a squatter. Unfortunately for him, others claimed rights under an earlier Mexican land grant. A law suit ensued and lasted eighteen years before Campbell finally bought out the other parties. That land later became the city's historical downtown core. It slowly developed and became an important rail center for shipping fruit and other produce. A post office was established and Campbell became its first postmaster.

CARLOS, SAN

Tradition holds that the San Mateo County city got its name from one of three sources: 1) The ship *San Carlos* which entered San Francisco Bay in August, 1775 under the command of Lieutenant Juan Manuel de Ayala, who had been ordered to make a navigational chart of the bay on which future Spanish ships could rely; 2) for the King of Spain, Charles III; or 3) for Saint Charles, on whose feast day, November 4, 1769, the Portolá Expedition first discovered the bay. The saint, Charles Borromeo (1538-1584), was the archbishop of Milan, a Cardinal, and a leader of the Catholic reformation He is the patron saint of learning and the arts.

CARLSBAD

The San Diego coastal city is named after the famous spa town of Carlsbad in the Czech Republic ("Karlsbad" in German) which in turn is named for its founder, the Holy Roman Emperor Charles IV (1316-1378), "Karl" being German for "Charles." "Bad" refers to spa or springs. The California town was developed by the Carlsbad Land and Water Company in 1886 after the discovery of mineral springs there.

CARMICHAEL

Located between Sacramento and Fair Oaks, the community was named in 1910 after developer Daniel W. Carmichael (1867-1927) who in 1909 began selling his

Carmichael Colonies 10-acre lots for $1,500, with 10 percent down, $10 a month, 6% interest. He had come to Sacramento in 1885 from his native Georgia and within ten years had organized a real estate firm devoted to the development of the Sacramento Valley. He was also active in local politics and was elected treasurer for the city and the county of Sacramento in 1885 and 1903, respectively. He was mayor of Sacramento in 1917-18. He also served as a director for the Sacramento Chamber of Commerce for eighteen years. He left Sacramento about 1923 and reportedly lived in England before returning to live in San Francisco.

CARRILLO STATE PARK, LEO
Just north of Santa Monica on the Pacific Coast Highway, the park honors the actor and conservationist Leo Carrillo (1880- 1961). He was part of a Los Angeles family which could trace its roots back to the *conquistadores*. His great-grandfather was the first provisional governor of California. The family moved from San Diego to Los Angeles then to Santa Monica, where Leo's father served as the city's first mayor. In Hollywood, Carrillo appeared in more than ninety films in which he played supporting or character roles. However, he is best remembered from the television show the "Cisco Kid" on which he played Pancho, a role he had previously performed in several films. Carrillo served on the California Beach and Parks Commission for eighteen years and played a key role in the state's acquisition of Hearst Castle at San Simeon, the Los Angeles Arboretum, and the Anza-Borrego Desert State Park. As a result of his service to the State, the park was named in his honor, as was the **Leo Carrillo State Beach** in Malibu. **The Leo Carrillo Ranch Historic Park** in Carlsbad is a registered California Historical Site.

CARSON
In 1782 Juan José Dominguez (1736-1809) received the first land grant in California history—75,000 acres in Los Angeles' South Bay area, which he named *Rancho San Pedro*. Settlement remained sparse for over a century.

Dominguez's eldest son, Manuel (1803-1882), and his wife, María Engracia Cota, had ten children, six of whom survived, all daughters. One of them, María Victoria, married a young entrepreneur named George Henry Carson and moved into the *rancho's* Victorian house next to the original adobe of her grandfather. They had fifteen children, one of whom, John Manuel Carson (1862-1928), would play an important role in the development of the South Bay in the twentieth century. He and his uncle Gregorio del Amo were directors of the Dominguez Estate Company which controlled the land. In 1967, the company liquidated its assets after negotiating the largest real estate transaction in the history of Southern California at the time. It sold off 1600 acres of the original land grant for over $58 million. When the city was incorporated in 1968, the residents rejected the historical name of Dominguez in favor of Carson, in tribute to John Manuel Carson. The family name, however, continues in **Dominguez Hills**, a hilly area in Carson, the location of California State University, Dominguez Hills.

CARSON RIVER

The 150-mile-long river in northern California and northwestern Nevada is named for the famous scout Kit Carson (1809-1868). It was used during the 1850s and 1860s as the route of the Carson Trail, part of the California Trail that led to the gold fields. Born and raised in Missouri, at seventeen he left for New Mexico and the Rockies to work as a trapper. In 1842 he met John C. Frémont, who hired him as a guide, and for the next few years navigated him to Oregon and California. Frémont's popular reports of his expeditions soon made Carson a national hero, mythologizing him in the press and dime novels as an intrepid, almost superhuman, mountain man. In 1846, when Frémont joined the Bear Flag rebellion, Carson led the troops of General Kearney from New Mexico into California when Pico and his band challenged the American occupation of Los Angeles. At the end of the war, Carson returned to New Mexico and took up ranching. In 1867 he moved to Colorado in order to expand his ranching ventures. He died there the following year.

CASPAR

The small village and creek watershed in Mendocino County is named for the man who founded it in 1857, Siegfried Caspar, a German trapper who raised horses there. It is home to the **Caspar Headlands State Reserve** and **Caspar State Beach**

CASTRO, THE

This San Francisco neighborhood was originally called Eureka Valley. In the 1960s and '70s, gay men began moving in and the district soon was named for its main thoroughfare, Castro Street, named for José Antonio Castro (1808-1860). Born in Monterey, he served as the acting governor of Alta California from 1835 until 1836 after the death of Governor José Figueroa. Castro opposed the Mexican government's authority over Alta California and sought a semi-independent status for the territory. In 1836 he organized a revolt against his successor as Governor. He was appointed to the position of Lieutenant-Colonel of the California militia in 1837.

CASTROVILLE

The Central Coast town, the self-proclaimed "Artichoke Center of the World," was founded in 1863 by Juan Bautista Castro (1853-1915), the son of a Mexican soldier and early Monterey *alcalde* with important ties—his wife was the sister of Governor Pío Pico—which may be why his son was granted several large tracts of land. These were combined into the enigmatically-named *Rancho Bolsa Nueva y Moro Cojo* ("New Pocket and Lame Moor"). The southwest corner of the land became what is today Castroville. Juan Bautista was a newspaper editor, perennial office-seeker, and real estate promoter. He served as Monterey County Treasurer in the 1870s and County Supervisor in the 1890s. He was portrayed by some newspapers of the day as an ambitious, grasping Yankeefied successor to the quaint grandees of the old *ranchos.* On the other hand, his obituary in the Salinas newspaper stated: "Suavity and politeness of the old school style and whole-souled generosity were distinguishing characteristics with him. He always gave liberally to both religious and educational institutions, and was ever ready to help the needy."

CASTRO VALLEY
Guillermo Castro (1810-18??), a native Californian and career military officer, served in the Mexican army as a lieutenant of militia at the *pueblo* of San Jose. In 1838 he acquired a land grant, roughly forty-one square miles, then known as *Rancho San Lorenzo,* which included those areas that would become the cities of Hayward, San Lorenzo, and Castro Valley. He married early, to Luisa Peralta of the nearby *San Antonio Rancho,* and had seven children before he was thirty. In spite of his wealth in land and livestock, Castro fell prey to a weakness for high-stakes gambling, especially three-card monte, and was forced to sell off much of his land to pay debts. The remaining land ultimately had to be sold at a sheriff's sale in 1864; the buyer was Faxon Atherton. Castro and his family moved to Chile where they spent their remaining lives. His name is also commemorated by the **Don Castro Regional Recreation Area**, established in 1969.

CASWELL MEMORIAL STATE PARK
Thomas Caswell (1843-1927), an Irish immigrant, was a rancher and farm equipment manufacturer who, from 1901 to his death, lived in Ceres. He took ownership of the riparian forest that would become the park when he purchased 700 acres along the Stanislaus River near the town of Ripon in 1915. In accordance with his intention that the forest be preserved for future generations to enjoy, in 1950 the Caswell family donated 134 acres of forest to the state as a memorial to him and his sons, Wallace (1875-1950) and Charles Henry (1876-1949).

CATALINA ISLAND, SANTA
This Channel Island was first sighted by Vizcaíno on

November 24, 1602, the eve of St. Catherine's Day. As was the tradition for christening new places, it was named in her honor. Known as St. Catherine of Alexandria, according to legend the fourth-century martyr was converted to Christianity through a vision, after which she set about converting her countrymen. She denounced the Roman emperor Maxentius for his persecution of Christians; he retaliated by burning fifty of her converts at the stake. He then offered Catherine a royal marriage if she would deny her faith. She refused and was imprisoned. During her stay and while Maxentius was away, she converted his wife and two hundred of his soldiers. Upon his return, he discovered what she had done and had them all put to death. Catherine herself was put on a spiked wheel, and when the wheel broke, she was beheaded.

CERES

Ceres is the only city in California to be named after a goddess. In this case, the Roman goddess of agriculture. It is an appropriate appellation as the city, located in the central San Joaquin Valley in the heart of Stanislaus County, is in one of the region's richest agricultural areas.

CHABOT REGIONAL PARK, ANTHONY

Located on the eastern border of Oakland, it is named after the man who created its first water system. Born in Quebec in a family of sixteen children, Anthony Chabot (1814-1888) struck out on his own at an early age. In his thirties he heard of the discovery of gold in California and turned westward. When he arrived at Nevada City, the hub of gold mining activity, he considered trying to move dirt by means of water to get to the gold. He used "ground sluicing" instead of the methods used by other miners. It proved a success from the first, and he soon started up a hydraulic mining company, making as much as a thousand dollars a day using this method. As the first man to extract gold by means of moving the earth by water pressure, he was dubbed "the father of hydraulic mining." He built two saw mills in Sierra County. The lumber was used in building dams, flumes, and sluices for mines. After leaving the mines Chabot went to San Francisco and started the first public water system in that city. His success there led him to do the same for Oakland, badly in need of running water; at that time, it was supplied only by wells. He found a creek which he thought would be what was needed. Temescal Creek was dammed, a lake was formed, and by 1879 the city was supplied from Lake Temecsal.

Chabot's name was always among the first on the list whenever money was needed for charitable purposes. He gave most of the money for the building to house veterans in Yountville. He gave Oakland an observatory located in Lafayette Park. His last gift was the largest ever given to any Oakland charity, a residence for women out of work, and daycare for their children.

CHAVEZ RAVINE
The steep canyon in downtown Los Angeles, best known today as the site of Dodger Stadium, was named for Julian Chávez (1789-1879). In 1837 he came from his native New Mexico to Los Angeles, where he worked for Abel Stearns, southern California's biggest landowner at the time, and started accumulating land. In 1844 he was granted an 83-acre plot which would become known as Chavez Ravine.. He took an active role in politics, being elected to the Common Council and, in 1852, to the first County Board of Supervisors. He would go on be reelected nine times.

CHESTER
The small Plumas County community took its name from Chester, Vermont, which was named in 1766 for the Earl of Chester (George Augustus Frederick [1762-1830]), the eldest son of King George III, who would succeed his father as George IV.

CLARA, SANTA
Misión Santa Clara de Asís was founded on January 12, 1777 and named for Clare of Assisi (1194-1253), the founder of the Order of the Poor Clares. On the advice of Saint Francis, she withdrew to the convent of San Damiano in Assisi where she and her followers formed a new order,

devoted to work and prayer, penance and contemplation. The city and county of Santa Clara took their names from the Mission.

CLARITA, SANTA

This southland city in what used to be called the Newhall-Saugus area (named for Henry Newhall (1825-1882) and the Massachusetts city of his birth, respectively) is also named for the same saint as Santa Clara. In fact it was named first, by Portolá's expedition in 1769. When the party was coming down the mountains between what is now called the San Fernando Valley and the valley beyond, it forded a stream that they promptly named the Santa Clara River. Eight years later, the Franciscans established a mission south of San Francisco which they called Santa Clara. As time progressed the northern mission was surrounded by Santa Clara County and the city of Santa Clara, the southern stream began to be referred to as the "little Santa Clara River," that is, "Santa Clarita." That was the name chosen for the city when it was incorporated in 1987.

CLAYTON

The Contra Costa County town is named for the English-born Joel Clayton (1812-1872). At twenty-five he emigrated to the United States, first settling in Pennsylvania, before moving on to Missouri, Illinois, and Wisconsin, during which time he learned the rudiments of mining. In 1850, like so many other young men, he lighted out for California to strike it rich. Over the next several years he lived in Stockton and San Francisco, where he started a dairy farm. In 1856 he was joined by his wife and their three small children and settled at San Francisco Pass, thirty miles from Los Angeles. The following year his wanderings finally stopped with a move north to Diablo Valley where he founded and laid out the town of Clayton. He became a civic leader in the San Francisco Bay Area and one of the major landowners in Clayton. The toss of a coin is said to have decided whether the town would be named "Rhinesville" for his business partner, Charles

Rhine, or "Clayton" for its founder.

CLEMENTE ISLAND, SAN
The southernmost of the Channel Islands was named by Vizcaíno, who spotted it on November 23, 1602, Saint Clement's feast day. Saint Clement of Rome, also known as Pope Saint Clement, who lived during the first century, was the first Apostolic Father of the early Christian Church. Almost nothing is known of his life and death.

CLEVELAND NATIONAL FOREST
The almost 400,000-acre Cleveland National Forest is the southernmost National Forest in the state. It was originally set aside in 1893 to protect the health of the watersheds from erosion damage and flooding that followed forest wildfires. It was designated a National Forest in 1908 by President Theodore Roosevelt and named in honor of President Grover Cleveland (1837-1908), the man whose portrait adorns the face of the $1,000 bill, who had ten years earlier established the San Jacinto Forest Reserve (subsumed by the new National Forest) and had died a week before the naming.

CLOVIS
In the midst of the San Joaquin Valley in Fresno County, since its incorporation in 1912 Clovis has been known as the "Gateway to the Sierra." Its namesake is Clovis M. Cole (1859-1939), a man who spent nearly all of his life in the area. Son of a prominent Fresno businessman, he was born in Indiana, but grew up on his father's homestead which became the town of Clovis. When he was sixteen, his father gave him four horses so that he could become a teamster, hauling lumber from the mountains. By the time he was twenty-five, he and an uncle grew more wheat than anyone else in California--so much so that he became known as "The Wheat King." In 1891 the San Joaquin Valley Railroad reached Cole's property and bought a right-of-way from him and agreed to build a station and call it "Clovis." From this sprang the town.

COBB

John Cobb (1814-1893) came to California in 1853 from his native Kentucky and homesteaded north of Napa Valley, towards Clear Lake in what is today Lake County, and settled in a place now known as Cobb Valley, which took his name. In 1854 he was elected Napa County Assessor. He lived for about five years in Cobb Valley, then sold his land and moved to Napa Valley, at about the time Lake County was sectioned off from Napa County.

COE STATE PARK, HENRY W.

At over 87,000 acres, the largest state park in northern California, it is named for Henry Willard ("Harry") Coe, Jr. (1860-1943), whose Pine Ridge Ranch was owned by he and his family from 1905 to 1953. He was born in what is now San Jose and moved to the Santa Clara area when he was forty-five, homesteading land deep in the Diablo mountain range in the 1880s. He bought out neighboring homesteaders until his ranch ranged over 13,000 acres. There he managed a cattle operation and raised his children. Ten years after his death, his daughter, Sada, donated the ranch to Santa Clara County as park lands. In 1958 it became part of the state park system.

William E. Colby

COLBY MOUNTAIN

The 6000-foot mountain in Tehama County was named in 1909 for William E. Colby (1875-1964), a San Francisco attorney and mountaineer. He was a member of the Board of Directors of the Sierra Club for forty-nine years. He was instrumental in enlarging Sequoia and creating Kings Canyon and Olympic National Parks. He served as the first chairman of the California State Park Commission (1927-36). In 1961, he became the first recipient of the Sierra Club's John Muir Award. **Colby Meadow** was named for him in 1911 by members of the U.S. Forest Service engaged in building the John Muir Trail. **Colby Pass** was discovered by a Sierra Club party led by Colby in 1912. In 1928 **Colby Lake** was named for him.

COLFAX

Located in the Sierra foothills of Placer County, the town is named for the politician Schuyler Colfax (1823-1885), an ardent supporter of the transcontinental railroad. In 1865, while acting as Speaker of the House of Representatives, he visited the location and the railroad station, and, later, the community, was named for him. Colfax was a close friend of President Lincoln and was at the White House on the evening when Lincoln left for Ford's Theater. He was invited by the President to accompany him, but declined. Three years later Colfax was elected Vice-President under Grant. A controversial figure, in 1872 he was embroiled in the Credit Mobilier scandal. Due to corruption charges, Colfax was not renominated as Grant's Vice-President. Periodically, there have been efforts to remove Colfax's name from the city due to this notorious career; all have failed.

COLTON

About fifty miles east of Los Angeles, in San Bernardino County, it is named after David D. Colton (1831-1878). Born in Maine and raised in Illinois, at nineteen he answered the siren song of gold and headed to California with a friend. Eventually he got into railroading and became vice-president of the Southern Pacific Railroad. In 1874 he and Charles Crocker, the line's president, attended a meeting in San Bernardino. Residents there wanted the railroad to pass through the city but such a line would have been off the most direct route and prohibitively expensive to maintain. A stretch of land southwest of the city was the most likely site for the location of a train station and so the town of Colton came to be. The town site is said to have been named by the railroad to honor Colton, but some have suggested that Colton himself named the town. Residing in San Francisco, Colton built one of the most elaborate residences ever seen in the city on Nob Hill. The classic white wooden mansion featured an entry flight of marble steps leading to a great portico of Corinthian columns. He, his wife, and their two daughters entertained there in splendor. He was a friend of Senator Broderick and acted as his second in the latter's fatal duel with Justice Terry in 1853. He died at the age of forty-seven when his horse fell on him at his Mount Diablo Ranch. Shortly thereafter, his widow closed the house and moved to Washington, D.C.

COMPTON

The city, located at what had once been part of the *Rancho San Pedro*, originally granted to Juan José Dominguez, started as a stop on the route of the region's first rail line--Los Angeles-San Pedro Railroad—completed in 1869. It was incorporated in 1888 and named for Griffith D. Compton (1820-1905), founder of a Methodist temperance college there. He was born in Virginia and as a young man moved westward, living in Illinois and Iowa before taking the overland route to Sacramento in 1849, where he tried his hand at mining, then finally settled in Nevada for thirteen years before moving permanently to Los Angeles where he grew wealthy. Interested in higher education, he was one of the first trustees of the University of Southern California.

COOLBRITH, MOUNT INA

The first librarian of the Oakland Free Library (1878), where she served as a mentor to young Jack London, and later California's first poet laureate, Ina Coolbrith (1841-

1928) came with her parents to California in 1852 from St. Louis in an ox-drawn "prairie schooner" through Beckwourth Pass. She was so well regarded that on the day of her funeral the State Legislature adjourned in her memory and afterward named the 8,000-foot peak near Beckwourth Pass "Mount Ina Coolbrith."

CORCORAN

Incorporated in 1914, and located in the heart of the San Joaquin Valley in Kings County, the city is not certain about the provenance of its name. Its own website claims that it was named after a railroad superintendent named Thomas Corcoran or an early steamboat captain named Michael Corcoran. However, there is evidence that it might very well have been named after two brothers, Bernard Corcoran (1849-1926) and Thomas Corcoran (1851-19??). Bernard, who never married, had a successful business career in California, and had acquired considerable wealth. Thomas, who, like Bernard, had emigrated from Ireland to Visalia in the early 1870s to join their sister Mary and her husband, George McCann, was manager of the McCann ranch from 1889 to 1920. The Corcoran brothers gave a right of way to the Santa Fe Railway to pass through a property which they owned. In return the company agreed to name the railway station at the site for them, which in time grew to became the city of Corcoran.

CORCORAN, MOUNT

The 13,747-foot mountain is part of the Le Conte massif located on the Sierra Crest. It seems that in 1878 the German-American Hudson River artist Albert Bierstadt (1830-1902) painted what had been known as Sheep Mountain (know called Mount Langley) in the Sierra. Wanting to patronize the renowned East Coast art patron William Wilson Corcoran (1798-1888), the painter changed the landscape's name from the generic "Mountain Lake" to "Mt. Corcoran." This confusion continued until 1937 when it was officially dubbed Mt. Langley. Not until 1968, however, was the name "Corcoran" officially applied, perhaps as a consolation, to its present site (once called "Old Mount Whitney"), adjacent to Langley.

CORDELIA

This area of Fairfield (at the northern end of San Francisco Bay), the Solano County seat, was named for Cordelia Sterling Waterman (1813-1885), wife of Robert "Bully" Waterman, a clipper ship captain who had sailed around the world five times and had set the sailing record from China to New York (74 days) in 1849 aboard his *Sea Witch*. In 1850 he moved to Suisun Valley where he raised cattle from Texas and grew lima beans to sell to Gold Rush miners. He had purchased a third of the *Suisun Rancho*, which had been granted to Chief Solano and his people by the Mexican government in 1837. Waterman dreamt of founding a great town. He selected the site of Cordelia as being suitable to that end. He first named the town Bridgeport, apparently in honor of his wife's hometown in Connecticut. It was subsequently changed to Cordelia because there was already a Bridgeport in Alpine County and the postal service would have demanded the change In 2001, the International Bird Rescue Research Center opened the San Francisco Bay Oiled Wildlife Care and Education Center in Cordelia.

CORNING

The Tehama County town, known as "Olive City" for its many ripe-olive canneries, is situated two hours north of Sacramento. It was laid out in 1882 by the Pacific Improvement Co., a subsidiary of the Central Pacific Railroad, and named in the memory of John Corning (1826-1878), Assistant Superintendent of the Railroad, who had died four years earlier. Hailing from Troy, New York, the nephew of the president of the New York Central Railroad, he began his railroading career at the age of thirty-two on the Michigan Central Railroad. Three years later, he was hired by his uncle to work for the New York Central Railroad. In 1868 he left to become Assistant Superintendent of the Central Pacific.

COTTLE STATE RECREATION AREA, MARTIAL

The Santa Clara County property was originally part of the extensive *Rancho de Santa Teresa* land holdings granted to the José Joaquin Bernal family by the Mexican governor in 1834. In 1864 Edward Cottle, who had immigrated to the area a decade earlier, purchased a portion of the *rancho* to farm and settle his family. He later deeded 350 acres to his son Martial Cottle (1833-1909), who used the property for growing crops and raising cattle and horses. After his death the ranch stayed in the family until 2004 when the sole remaining heir transferred 137 acres of the site to the state.

COULTERVILLE

In 1850 George W. Coulter (1827-1902) arrived in the Mariposa County gold fields and opened a store by the Merced River, where there were rich placers. Shortly afterwards, he heard that there were a great many miners on Maxwell's Creek and securing more goods moved to a tent and opened a "store" for business. A town grew around it, which was called Banderita, meaning "flag," so-named from an American flag which Coulter always had flying above his tent. A post-office was soon established, which was first called Maxwell's Creek but the citizens changed it in 1872 to Coulterville, in honor of its popular founder.. In the sixties he built a two story hotel to handle tourist travel. Water for this hotel was pumped from a well by two Newfoundland dogs. He died at Chinese Camp in Tuolomne County.

COURTLAND

The Sacramento River Delta town was founded in 1871 by James Valentine Sims (1828-1899) and named for his son Courtland. (1864-1919), one of his seven children. Sims had come to California with only the clothes on his back from Illinois in 1851. He worked hard for a few years until he was able to buy a hundred acres near Paintersville. He served as postmaster and as a Sacramento County Supervisor (1871-1874).

COWELL REDWOODS STATE PARK, HENRY

In 1849 Henry Cowell (1819-1903) left his Massachusetts home town to strike it rich in California. He started a drayage business which grew to include routes to Stockton and the gold country. Soon his "empire" grew to include property and business interests from San Luis Obispo to Washington State. With the population boom of the Gold Rush came the construction of towns and cities. Lime, made from processing limestone in wood-fired kilns, was high in demand and soon attracted Cowell's attention. In 1865 he got into the business in Santa Cruz. He bought ships, established a cement trade with Belgium and bought large land holdings, ranches, and limestone deposits in 23 California counties. He was so successful that in 1886 he was reported to have the highest income in Santa Cruz County. By 1899 he owned 10,000 acres of land. By 1900 the demand for lime began to decline and cement began to replace it. The business closed its doors for good in 1946. Cowell's youngest son, S.H. ("Harry") Cowell (1860-1955) was the last link in the family line. Two years before his death, S.H., in accordance with his desire that the redwoods on the property be preserved, negotiated with the County and the State, to create the Cowell Redwoods State Park on the San Lorenzo River near Felton, in memory of his father.

COWLES MOUNTAIN

San Diego's tallest peak takes its name from George Cowles 1836-1887)—pronounced "Coals." Prior to coming to California, he had been a successful cotton broker in New York. In 1871 he began purchasing large parcels of land in the El Cajon Valley, before ultimately settling there two years later to start a new career as a rancher on what totaled 4,000 acres. He planted many varieties of fruit trees, finding his greatest success in raisins—he became "America's Raisin King." The community that developed around the area where his home was became known first as Cowlestown, then Santee. Cowles also was active in local banking, drydocking, and served as a director of the California Southern Railroad.

CRESSEY
Calvin J. Cressey (1830-1891) was born and raised in New Hampshire and like so many of his contemporaries felt the urge to go West, coming to California where he acquired a large fortune, consisting mainly of extensive land holdings and controlling interests in two banks, the Modesto Bank and the Grangers Bank of San Francisco. The small community of Cressey is located on land he owned in northern Merced County, named for him by the Atchison, Topeka and Santa Fe Railway when it opened a station there in 1910.

CROCKETT
This town on the Straits of Carquinez, about six miles below Martinez, in Contra Costa County, was started in 1867 when Thomas Edwards built his homestead on land bought the previous year from Judge J. B. Crockett (1808-1884). Crockett, who had been born in Kentucky of a Scottish-American family, became a lawyer there at twenty-two. He soon moved to Missouri where he founded the St. Louis *Intelligencer*, Arriving in California in 1852, he resumed practicing law, this time in San Francisco, In 1868 he was appointed to the California Supreme Court and in 1869 was elected to succeed himself for the ten-year term, which he served in full. The land that was to become Crockett was originally included in an 1842 Mexican land grant to Teodora Soto. In 1865 Crockett, acting as a lawyer, settled a case concerning a boundary dispute for Ms. Soto; for his fee, he was given a strip of land one mile long and three miles wide extending along the Carquinez Straits. To protect his ownership from squatters, Crockett invited his friend Thomas Edwards to farm his land., selling it to him several years later, and upon which the present town of Crockett developed. **Crockett Hills Regional Park** opened in 2006.

CROOKS PEAK

65

Hulda Crooks (1896-1997) at 91 had ascended 98 mountains including Japan's Mount Fuji which she climbed at age 65. She is known as "Grandma Whitney" for having climbed Mount Whitney twenty-three times. One of eighteen children of a Saskatchewan farming couple, she made her first Whitney ascent when she was 66. In 1991, she made her last trip up the mountain, which she often called "my mountain." That same year, a peak south of Whitney was named Crooks Peak. It took an act of Congress to override the U.S. Board of Geographic Names' refusal to make an exception to its rule against using the name of a living person.

CROWN MEMORIAL STATE BEACH, ROBERT
Robert Crown (1922-1973) was a Democratic Assemblyman from Alameda County from 1956 to his death from injuries suffered after being hit by a car while jogging. The beach was named in his memory because of his efforts to make it a public parkland, which became official in 1980.

CUDAHY
Michael Cudahy (1841-1910), born in County Kilkenny, Ireland, emigrated with his family to the United States in 1849 and settled in Milwaukee. After leaving school Cudahy found work as a meat-packer. With his brother John and Philip Armour he started his own meat-packing business in Omaha, Nebraska. In the 1870s he revolutionized the industry by introducing summer curing under refrigeration. In 1908, Cudahy sold his share of the company and bought a 2,800 acre ranch east of Los Angeles. He subdivided it into long and narrow one-acre lots which were referred to as "Cudahy Acres," and were marketed as small ranches. The concept attracted people from the midwest who desired to own their own farm land. These farmers became Cudahy's core settlers in the mid-1920s. The community became incorporated in 1960 as Cudahy.

CULL CANYON

In 1849 William Slead Cull (1829-1896) left his Kentucky home and crossed the plains, settling in Alameda County in what is now Castro Valley at what he named Cull Canyon. Little by little he added to his ranching land, so that it exceeded over a thousand acres at his death. The area is home to **Cull Creek**, **Cull Canyon Reservoir**, and **Cull Canyon Regional Recreation Area**.

CULVER CITY

The earliest European settlement of the area, eleven miles west of downtown Los Angeles, was *Rancho La Ballona,* Real estate developer and promoter Harry Hazel Culver (1880-1946) bought and subdivided part of it and got early filmmakers to build studios there that later became MGM. Culver was born on a Nebraska farm. At thirteen he enlisted in the Spanish-American War, after which he attended college for a few years.. From 1901 to about 1904 he worked in the Philippines in the mercantile business and as a reporter for the *Manila Times*. He began working in real estate in Southern California in 1910 for I.N. Van Nuys. In 1913 in a speech at the California Club in Los Angeles Culver announced his plans for what was to become Culver City, saying that "If you draw a straight line from [downtown's] Story building to the oceanfront at Venice, at the halfway mark you will find three intersecting electric lines--the logical center for a town site." Local voters rejected the land's annexation to Los Angeles in 1914, whereupon Culver founded the Culver Investment Company, which began as a campaign with the slogan "All roads lead to Culver City" and began to bus in potential lot purchasers. Culver City became incorporated in 1917 with a population of 530.

CUPERTINO

John T. Doyle, a San Francisco lawyer, bought a vineyard and house in 1873 in what was then called Stevens Creek. Interested in local history, he learned that the famous De Anza expedition of the 1770's had passed through the area and that its cartographer/diarist, Pedro Font, had named the creek *Arroyo de San Jose de Cupertino*. His enthusiasm for the name caught on, so when the Home Union Store was incorporated as the Cupertino Union Store in 1904, the Post Office, located within the store, also changed its designation to Cupertino.

San Giuseppe da Copertino (1603-1663) was born Giuseppe Desa. He received the "Cupertino" from the name of a small village in the Kingdom of Naples, near where the Franciscan friary he was associated with lies. His claim to fame was that he would get so caught up in his prayers that he would levitate and fly around the room, While there are more than 200 Catholic saints who have been known to levitate, Desa's are known as the most extraordinary, which is perhaps why he became known as the patron saint of aviators. Unfortunately, because of these uncontrollable levitations and public ecstatic trances, Desa was not allowed to celebrate Mass in public, sing in the choir, or attend processions. He was canonized in 1767 as "Saint Joseph of Cupertino."

D

DALY CITY

John Daly (1840-1923) left Boston for California at the age of thirteen, accompanying his mother by ship. She died on the Panama crossing and the young man continued the journey alone, eventually finding work on a dairy farm in San Mateo County. By 1868 he had earned enough money to purchase about 250 acres at the "top-of-the-hill," south of San Francisco. He started the San Mateo Dairy and was soon supplying milk and its products from the dairy's own cows and from a consortium of other dairies. In the 1860s a railroad ran south to San Jose, near the edge of Daly's ranch, spawning businesses at the bottom of the hill. By the early 1890's streetcars were running from San Francisco to communities as far south as San Mateo, coming right over Daly's Hill, as a stop was appropriately named. Daly moved to San Francisco in 1885, but maintained his business at the "top-of-the-hill." He subdivided his property in 1907 and streets were quickly laid out. By 1911 there was enough support to incorporate. By a slim margin a new city was voted into being, named in honor of John Daly.

DANA, MOUNT

The mountain in Yosemite National Park was named by the Whitney Survey in 1863 for James Dwight Dana (1813-1895), at the time America's most eminent geologist, teaching at the famous Sheffield Scientific School at Yale. Dana was raised in Utica, New York, where he liked to "tramp" and collect rocks, plants, and insects. He trained in several scientific disciplines at Yale under his future father-in-law, Benjamin Silliman, founder and editor of the *American Journal of Science*. He became the geologist and mineralogist of the U.S. Exploring Expedition (1838-1842) charged with charting islands in the Pacific. It was the first American exploration on land or sea to make systematic geological observations.

Richard Henry Dana

DANA POINT

The City of Dana Point, incorporated in 1989, is named for the bay on which it is located which, in turn, is named for Richard Henry Dana Jr. (1815-1882), the Harvard-trained lawyer, seaman, and author of the classic journal *Two Years Before the Mast* (1840). In it Dana documented his voyage from Boston around Cape Horn to California on the merchant brig *Pilgrim*. He described the area known at the time as Capistrano Bay, as "the most romantic spot on the California coast." That bay was later rechristened Dana Point in the author's honor.

DANVILLE

The San Ramon Valley town was settled by Americans drawn there by the Gold Rush. Daniel Inman (1828-1908) and his brother, Andrew, bought 400 acres of what is now "Old Town" Danville with their mining earnings in 1854, after living there for a summer two years earlier. By 1858, the community boasted a blacksmith, a hotel, a wheelwright and a general store and the townsfolk wanted a post office. With regard to the name, the Inman brothers rejected "Inmanville," finally settling on Danville. According to the modest Dan, the name was chosen as much or more out of respect for Andrew's mother-in-law who was born and raised near Danville, Kentucky. The Kentucky town was founded in 1781 by a young lawyer from Virginia, Walker Daniel, who bought seventy-six acres and had it surveyed as a town site in 1783- He was killed by Indians the following year and the town was named in his honor. Daniel Inman moved to Livermore and went on to serve on the Alameda County Board of Supervisors (1867-68, the State Assembly (1869), and as an elected representative to the convention that revised the original California Constitution in 1878-79.

DAVENPORT

The small beach town just north of Santa Cruz is named for Captain John Davenport (1818-1892), a whaler originally from Rhode Island. He moved permanently to Monterey where he resided in the first brick house in California. There he started the first coastal whaling enterprise, before moving it to the Santa Cruz area where in 1868 he built a wharf ("Davenport's Landing") and the village of Davenport quickened into life. Whaling turned out not to be profitable and in 1880 the wharf was abandoned and the Captain moved to Santa Cruz.

DAVIDSON, MOUNT

At 938 feet above sea level, Mt. Davidson is the highest geographic point on the San Francisco skyline and home to the largest cross in the world. It was originally named

Blue Mountain in 1852 by the English-born George Davidson (1825-1911), a geographer and astronomer who served as Chief of the U.S. Coast and Geodetic Survey's Pacific Operations. At Davidson's death, it was renamed for him at the urging of the Sierra Club in honor of his charter membership and significant scientific achievements.

DAVIS

Founded in 1868, the Central Valley city was originally named Davisville for Jerome C. Davis (1822-1880), a local farmer whose ranch became the site for the town. The Davisville post office shortened the town name in 1907 and it was made official when the city incorporated in 1917. Davis was born and raised in Ohio and traveled overland as a member of Frémont's topographical survey expedition which arrived in California in 1845. He settled in Sacramento and briefly tried his luck with mining at the start of the Gold Rush, but decided he could better capitalize on it in other ways, such as a rope ferry across the Sacramento River. Prices were so inflationary at that time he could collect as much as $10,000 per month from the ferry tolls. He bought land and by 1864 had accumulated 13,000 acres. He also helped to establish the county's first dairy farm at a time when milk could be sold for a dollar per gallon. However, by 1863 the farm did not succeed due to crop failures, and most of it was sold off in 1868 to promoters of Davisville and the California Pacific Railroad which found it an ideal site for their expansions.

DELANO

Started up in 1873 as a railroad station, the name of the Kern County agricultural town was selected by the Southern Pacific Railroad to honor Columbus Delano (1809-1896), at the time the Secretary of the Interior under President Grant. The corruption that permeated much of Grant's administration became especially rampant in the Bureau of Indian Affairs during Delano's tenure, and it ultimately led to his resignation in 1875 when evidence surfaced that his son had been given partnerships in surveying contracts over which the Interior Department had control.

DEWITT REDWOODS STATE NATURAL RESERVE, JOHN B.

The Oakland-born, UC Berkeley-educated John Bolton Dewitt (1937-1996) served as Secretary and Executive Director of the Save-the-Redwoods League from 1971 to 1995. He was instrumental in obtaining more than $65 million in donations used to acquire 30,000 acres of park lands in Northern and Central California and rescuing the ancient redwood forests from destruction. The 578-acre reserve, established in 1991, is near the small southern Humboldt County town of Redway.

DIEGO, SAN

In 1542 Juan Rodríguez Cabrillo arrived in San Diego Bay and named it San Miguel after the saint whose feast day was closest to the landing. Sixty years later Sebastian Viscaíno, leading another Spanish expedition, entered the harbor and renamed it for San Diego de Alcalá de Henares (Spain) (1400-1463), known in English as Saint Didicus, because it was that saint's feast day. *San Diego* was also the name of the flagship for this expedition. The saint became a Franciscan lay brother at an early age. He was sent to the Canary Islands to convert the infidels. Later, in Rome, during an epidemic he attended the sick, restoring many to health by, it was reported, making the sign of the cross over them. He spent his last decades in his native Spain doing good works.

DIMAS, SAN

The early settlement that preceded San Dimas was called Mud Springs and, briefly, Mound City. As local legend has it, Don Ygnacio Palomares, who received the *Rancho San José* as part of a land grant, kept some of his cattle in a corral in Horsethief Canyon. After Native Americans ran his horses off, he prayed to St. Dimas, the crucified thief who begged forgiveness for his sins and later became patron saint of reformed thieves. Soon the canyon was

73

renamed San Dimas Canyon by Spanish settlers, and when the town was laid out in 1887, after the railroad came through, the founders took the name, which sounded better than "Mud Springs" and would therefore be more likely to attract new residents. Saint Dimas, usually known as Saint Dismas, was the unnamed "good thief" that was crucified at Jesus's side, according to the Gospel of Luke. Unlike other saints, he was never actually canonized by the Roman Catholic Church, but is held to be a saint because Jesus said, according to tradition, that he would be in Paradise.

DISNEYLAND PARK
The 85-acre theme park in Anaheim, named for, and conceived by, the Great Animator, Walt Disney (1901-1966), opened in 1955. In 1939 he became an investor in the Sugar Bowl resort near Donner Pass in Placer County. Its principal slope was renamed **Mount Disney** (elev. 7943 feet) in his honor and was the site of the first chair-lift in California.

DIXON
The first settlement in the Dixon area was founded in 1852 by Elijah S. Silvey, whose search for gold landed him in the area during the Gold Rush. When the Vaca Valley railroad was about to inaugurate its new line in Solano County in 1870. the residents of Silveyville were not pleased when they discovered that the tracks would not cross into their town; they did, however, cross the land of rancher Thomas Dickson (1800-1885). In order for the town to grow, the residents of Silveyville would have to move closer to the tracks. With Dickson in charge of the re-location, the buildings were moved on large flat cars with wooden rollers to the railroad tracks. The California Pacific Railroad tracks were almost finished and a train station was needed. Dickson donated ten acres of his land for the depot if the town would be called Dicksonville. The first rail shipment of merchandise arrived in 1872 mistakenly addressed to "Dixon" and that spelling stuck. In 1874, after nearly a two-year push to have the town named

Dicksonville, the County Recorder filed maps with the name Dixon, stating it was "simpler."

DOCKWEILER STATE BEACH
Isidore B. Dockweiler (1867-1947) was a prominent Los Angeles lawyer and Democratic Party stalwart, as well as an unsuccessful candidate for Lieutenant Governor and U.S. Senator. Both his father and his son were distinguished lawyers as well. He served as president of the Los Angeles Public Library and on the State Board of Parks and Beaches. In 1955 the Venice-Hyperion Beach was renamed the Dockweiler State Beach in his honor.

DOHENY STATE BEACH PARK
In 1931 Edward Doheny (1856-1935) donated forty-one acres of ocean-front property in Dana Point to the State of California to be used "perpetually for public use." Known today as Doheny State Beach Park, it was California's first state beach. Subsequent land acquisitions from the Santa Fe Railroad, University of California Regents, and Union Oil Company added an additional twenty-one acres.

Doheny was possessed of an immense ambition. He was drawn to the West from his native Wisconsin to seek his fortune. He failed at prospecting before discovering oil in a noisome lot in Los Angeles in 1892. Confident that it had commercial value, he had visions of trains and ships being powered by oil instead of coal. After setting up huge oil wells in Mexico, he built an oil empire that made him one of the richest men in the world. But in 1924 the Teapot Dome scandal touched him. As the charges were filed, he hired the country's best lawyers to defend him. During the ten-year-long litigation Doheny's only son, Ned, was mysteriously murdered by a family friend. The government's case against Doheny ended in the jury acquitting him, while finding the cabinet official accused of taking a bribe from Doheny guilty. Notwithstanding the verdict, the scandal had cast its shadow over his many achievements and he died in disgrace.

75

DONNER LAKE

The lake, as well as the **Donner Pass** and **Donner Peak**, are named for the infamous Donner party, a group of wagon-train emigrants led by George Donner (1784?-1847) and his brother Jacob, who became trapped in the Sierra Nevada mountains during the winter of 1846-47. Nearly half of the party died, and some resorted to eating their dead in an effort to survive. The experience has become the stuff of legend in the record of Western migration.

DON PEDRO RESERVOIR

The reservoir was created from the dam built by the Modesto and Turlock Irrigation Districts about a mile below **Don Pedro Bar**, which got its name from a *don* of Spanish descent, who was from Mexico or Chile. Long before the Gold Rush reached the area, he is said to have taken numerous donkey loads of gold out of the area. In the 1850s, the gorges of the Tuolumne River, including Don Pedro Bar, Red Mountain Bar and Six Bit Gulch proved to be one of the richest placer- mining areas in the world. The town of Don Pedro Bar quickly sprang up in 1860 but was destroyed by fire four years later. With the gold fever dying, it never was restored. By the time the Don Pedro Dam and Reservoir were built, the only remnants of the once-lively town were a few fire-blackened chimneys, a cemetery with about thirty graves, only seven of which were marked with headstones, and one resident.

DORRIS

The city in Siskiyou County's Butte Valley is named for Presley Alexander Dorris (1822-1901) who started a stock-raising operation at what he called the "D" Ranch in 1862. When the railroad came through in 1907, the town was established and took Dorris' name. It was incorporated the following year.

DOWNEY

John Gately Downey (1827-1894) sailed to America from

his native Ireland in 1842. He came to California during the Gold Rush., eventually settling in Los Angeles where he invested in real estate and became involved in politics, which lead to his election as Lieutenant Governor in 1859. When Governor Latham resigned after five days in office to become a U.S. Senator, Downey became the state's seventh governor, the first from southern California. The Civil War began during his administration, with opponents viewing him, unfairly, as a secessionist favoring the South. As a result he was defeated when he ran for reelection. Downey was also responsible for developing Santa Fe Springs and Norwalk and was a founder of the Farmers and Merchants Bank, that later became part of Security Pacific Bank, which later merged with Bank of America. In November 1859, Downey and his partner, James McFarland, bought the 17,602 acre *Rancho Santa Gertrudes* in Los Angeles County for $60,000. In 1873, a 96-acre piece of it became the central district of a community called "Downey City," incorporated in 1956.

DOWNIEVILLE

Settled in late 1849, it is named after Major William Downie (1820-1893), a Scotsman who led the first expedition up the North Fork of the Yuba River. His travels are documented in his 1893 autobiography, *Hunting for Gold*. Downieville reached a peak population of over 5,000 people in 1851, before going into decline. It was nearly voted the state capital of California in 1853 before it was moved to Benicia, and then to Sacramento. Downieville has the dubious distinction of being the town where the only woman ever to be hung in the state took place. Juanita, a young Mexican woman, was found guilty of murder, convicted the same day it happened and was promptly hanged to a beam of the bridge over the Yuba River.

Sir Francis Drake

DRAKES BAY

The coast was reputedly visited by Sir Francis Drake (1540-1596) in 1579 during his circumnavigation of the world (1577–80). The name "Drakes Bay," as applied to the open roadstead that lies below Point Reyes, a few miles north of the Golden Gate, has nothing to do with Drake's whereabouts, as was pointed out by historian H.H. Bancroft in the 1880's. Apparently what happened is that the Spanish, as a result of their infrequent early voyages along the north coast, produced a rough map of the coastline in the early years of the seventeenth century, long before the discovery of San Francisco Bay. However, the bay below what is now called Point Reyes, was known to the Spanish, and on this map they labeled it the Bay of Saint Francis (in Spanish). Subsequently, a version of this map reached England and was published by a promoter of English expansion who, it seems, as a patriotic flourish, altered the name of the bay on the map to *Puerto de Francisco Draco* (creating in the process a Spanish- sounding name that no Spanish-speaking person would have made up, Drake being their country's hated enemy). When this was translated back into English, it became "Drakes Bay."

By the bay, and part of the Point Reyes National Seashore, are **Drake's Estero** and **Drake's Beach**.

DUARTE

Andres Duarte (1805-1863), born at Mission San Juan

Capistrano, at sixteen followed his father's career and joined the Mexican army. He was assigned to Mission San Gabriel. Gradually he assumed more responsibility and was finally the *mayordomo*, responsible for monitoring the outer lands of the Mission.. In 1841, on retirement from military service after 20 years, he petitioned Governor Juan Alvarado for a grant of land that was a vacant portion of the *Rancho Azusa* in the San Gabriel Valley. Within two weeks it was granted to him. In the mid-1850's he was unable to pay the property taxes and began to sell off his holdings, as his ranching operations failed to raise sufficient cash, a common problem for those who were rich in real estate. The ranching days of *Rancho Azusa de Duarte* ended, passing through several hands until it was subdivided into forty-acre parcels in the early 1870's. It remained primarily an agricultural area until after World War II, when it was largely converted into a residential community. In 1957 it was incorporated as the City of Duarte.

DUME, POINT

The peninsula in Malibu—part of it is now a State Preserve in Los Angeles County--is shown as "Point Duma" on older maps, and is actually named Point Dumetz, for Francisco Dumetz (17??-1811), the priest who founded the San Fernando mission. He was a native of Majorca, Spain, where he entered the Franciscan Order. In 1770 he went to Mexico with forty-eight other Franciscans to join the famous missionary college of San Fernando in the City of Mexico. On volunteering for the Indian missions, he was sent to California's Mission San Diego. In 1782 he was assigned to Mission San Buenaventura until 1797 when he was directed to found Mission San Fernando where he remained until 1805. From January, 1806, to the time of his death, Father Dumetz was stationed at San Gabriel.

DUNCANS MILLS

Two brothers from Scotland, Samuel and Alexander Duncan, started a sawmill in 1860 on the Russian River.

When the railroad line reached its north bank in 1877, Alexander towed his mill and other town buildings up river on a raft to the new site which was then called Duncans Mills. During that time and into the 1890's the brothers logged the redwoods which were sent by boat to San Francisco to build its wooden Victorians. Sam left, but Alexander remained to build a lumber empire.

DUNSMUIR

Early surveys determined that the upper Sacramento River Canyon was the most viable route for a railroad linking California with Oregon. In the mid-1880s the railroad entered Siskiyou County. Its camp was first called Pusher for the helper or pusher engines that were based there to assist trains over the steep grades to the north. Legend has it that shortly afterward, Alexander Dunsmuir (1853-1900), the son of the British Columbia "coal baron" Robert Dunsmuir, passed through and promised the settlers a fountain if they would name the place for him; his offer was accepted and the station, consisting of a boxcar, was duly christened Dunsmuir. The following year it was moved to Pusher and Dunsmuir followed through on his promise and the fountain was built near the station where it stands today. Alexander Dunsmuir moved to the San Francisco Bay Area from British Columbia in 1878 to manage his father's coal business. In 1899, he purchased 600 acres in the Oakland hills on which he built an elaborate 37-room mansion for his bride, Josephine. Neither ever got to enjoy it: Dunsmuir died while on his honeymoon, and his widow the following year.

E

EBBETTS PASS

Most accounts record that "Major" John Ebbetts (1817-1854) first identified this route in the early 1850's while leading a mule team over the Alpine County pass. In 1853 Ebbetts led a survey party back into the vicinity of the pass named for him in an attempt to locate a possible route for a transcontinental railroad into California from the east. It was not until later in the decade, with the discovery of silver on the east side of the Sierra, that merchants from the Gold Rush town of Murphys located and financed the present route through Ebbetts Pass. The road was built from west to east to truck freight and supplies to the silver mines and boom towns on the "east side."

EDWARDS AIR FORCE BASE

Northeast of Lancaster in the Antelope Valley and comprising over 300,000 acres, it was founded in 1933 and renamed (from Muroc Air Force Base) in 1949 to honor Capt. Glen W. Edwards (1918-1948), who was killed a year earlier when his YB-49 flying wing prototype bomber broke apart during a test flight. A medal-winning pilot during World War II he became a test pilot afterwards, earning a Master of Science degree in aeronautical engineering from Princeton in 1947.

EDWARDS SAN FRANCISCO BAY NATIONAL WILDLIFE REFUGE, DON

The nation's first urban wildlife refuge, 18,000 acres of wetlands at the south end of the Bay, honors former Congressman Don Edwards (b 1915) who served in the House of Representatives from 1963 to 1995. He was born William Donlon Edwards in San Jose and attended Stanford where he earned a law degree. Edwards led a difficult fight in Congress to enact the legislation and it was finally signed into law in 1972.

ELIGIO LAGOON, SAN

One of San Diego's largest coastal wetlands, the area was originally named *San Alejo* in honor of Saint Alexius by the Portolå Expedition in 1769. It is now part of the **San Elijo Lagoon Natural Preserve.** The name is also found in **San Elijo Hills**, a planned community in San Marcos, and **San Elijo State Beach**. Saint Alexius (13??-1417) was the son of a prominent Roman who, on the eve of his marriage, fled to the Near East where he lived as an ascetic for seventeen years. He then returned to Rome, where he lived for a like number of years as a beggar under the stairs of his father's palace, unknown to his father. After his death, a document was found on his person that revealed his true identity. He was immediately honored as a saint and his father's house was turned into a church.

EMERSON, MOUNT

John Muir was thirty-three-years old when he met the philosopher/poet Ralph Waldo Emerson (1803-1882) in Yosemite during the latter's stay in California in 1871. Emerson's health was in decline and the California trip was arranged partly to revitalize him. Writing to his wife from California, Emerson suggested that, if he were young, he might stay for good. California was for America a "new garden" and represented for him the future. The meeting with Emerson had a profound effect on Muir; he named the 13,225-foot mountain for him during a trip into Humphreys Basin in 1873.

EMERYVILLE

The New Hampshire-born Joseph S. Emery (1820-18??) came to California in 1850 by ship. He was a stone cutter who briefly visited the promising gold mines and then moved to the Bay Area. He returned to his original profession, quarrying rock on Angel and Goat Islands to erect the buildings that make up San Francisco's skyline. In 1859 Emery moved his home to the East Bay and purchased 185 acres of land north of Oakland for $8,000, calling it Emeryville and building the San Pablo Avenue Horse Cart Railroad connecting Emeryville to Oakland. He was also part of the group which organized the California-Nevada Railroad which began in Oakland and terminated in Orinda.

EMIGDIO MOUNTAINS, SAN

Before this traverse mountain range in Southern California was named, there were **San Emigdio Creek** and **San Emigidio Valley**, then the *Rancho San Emigdio*, a Mexican land grant in Kern County, first described in 1824. It is named after Saint Emygdius (c. 278-c. 309), a German pagan who converted to Christianity and became a bishop and, as tradition has it, suffered martyrdom in Italy. He is the patron saint of earthquakes.

ETIWANDA

In 1878 George Chaffey moved to Riverside from his Ontario home to join other Canadian families in the Santa Ana River irrigation settlement. He was joined by his sons, William and George, Jr. The large profits that flowed from the venture encouraged the brothers to become partners in the new irrigation colonies, named by them Etiwanda and Ontario, on the Cucamonga Plain. The name of the former was selected because they wanted to secure the interest of their Canadian friends in the venture and thought that the colony should have name pleasing to them. Etiwanda, a popular Lake Michigan Indian chief who had good business relations with their family, was chosen. In addition to his innovative irrigation schemes, George became interested in electric lighting. He was president and joint engineer of the Los Angeles Electric Company, which gave to that city the most extensive electrical lighting in the country at the time. He also set up the first trunk line telephones in California. There is an **Etiwanda Peak** (elev. 8862) in the Cucamonga Wilderness.

ETTERBURG

The Humboldt County town was named after Ettersburg, Germany, the ancestral home of Albert F. Etter (1872-1954), the founder of the California town. He had been born at Shingle Springs in Eldorado one of eleven children. In 1876 the family moved to Coffee Creek and later to Salt River, south of Eureka in the Eel River Valley. In 1894 he filed a homestead claim to five hundred acres at Ettersburg and it was here that he established the fruit-breeding farm and nursery which subsequently supplied new genetic material to breeders and growers around the world.

F

FAIRFAX

When Domingo Sais was mustered out of the Mexican Army in 1838, the government granted him almost 7,000 acres of land on what was then called *Cañada de Herrera* in Marin County. He gave a piece of it to Alfred W. Taliaferro, one of the first Europeans to settle in the area and the county's first physician, who, in 1855, gave 32 acres to his friend Charlie Fairfax (1829-1869) as a marriage gift. Fairfax and his wife built an estate, "Bird's Nest Glen," and lived there for thirteen years. Fairfax was sometimes known as the "The Baron," as he was in fact of Scottish noble descent and entitled to the title of 10th Lord Fairfax of Cameron. Charles left his home in Virginia when he was twenty to seek his fortune in the California gold fields. Not finding any, he turned to politics to make a living, first in 1851 as the head of the Marysville Committee of Vigilance. then as a member of the California State Assembly where he served as Speaker for a year, then Clerk of the State Supreme Court in 1856. After his move to Marin County, he became a County

Supervisor in 1865. In 1869, after traveling to New York as a delegate to the National Democratic Convention, he unexpectedly died at his mother's home in Baltimore.

FELTON
Born in Saugus, Massachusetts, after graduating Phi Beta Kappa from Harvard in 1847, John Brooks Felton (1827-1877) headed out to California where he started up a law firm with some of his former law school classmates. He became a mayor of Oakland (1869-1871), a University of California Regent (1868-1877). a judge, a twice unsuccessful candidate for the United States Senate, and a Bay Area investor. The Santa Cruz County town was laid out and given its name in 1868 by a San Francisco lawyer and former U.S. Congressman named Edward Stanly, who had bought the former Mexican land grant *Rancho Zayante* on which Felton is situated. Just what the relationship between he and Felton was that would move him to name the town after him is not known, though he is known to have been a client of Felton.

FERMIN, POINT
The southernmost point in Los Angeles was named by British explorer George Vancouver in 1793 for Father Fermín Francisco de Lasuén (1736-1803) in gratitude of his hospitality at the Carmel mission. The Second President of the California Missions was born in Vitoria, Spain, joined the Franciscan order and was ordained in 1752. Desiring to serve in the New World, he volunteered for service in 1758 and arrived in Mexico in 1761. His first building of a mission was in Baja California in 1768. He was then transferred to Alta California in 1773, basing his service out of San Diego. De Lasuén became President of the Missions in 1785 and built substantially on the work of his predecessor, Father Junípero Serra. He founded nine of California's twenty-one missions.

FERNANDO, SAN
The Los Angeles county, city and valley are named for *Misión San Fernando Rey de España*, founded by Padre

Fermín Francisco de Lasuén. It was dedicated to Saint Ferdinand, King of Spain. (1198-1252). Fernando III, who reigned from 1217 to 1251, and under whose rule the crowns of Castile and Leon were united, was the founder of the Spanish Inquisition, and was canonized in 1671 by Pope Clement X.

FILLMORE
In the late 1880s the Southern Pacific Railroad arrived in Ventura County's Santa Clara River Valley to promote the area east of present-day Fillmore. However, the owners of the land were not willing to sell, so it moved west to the juncture of the Santa Clara River and Sespe Creek, and founded the new community, naming it for the SP's General Superintendent, Jerome A. Fillmore (1845-1902). He had started out working on his father's Pennsylvania farm when he became fascinated by trains, stealing rides on them and running away to work as a brakeman on a coal train. He worked his way up the ranks to become General Superintendent of the Central and Southern Pacific railway system and was recognized as one of the finest such managers in the United States.

FIREBAUGH
This small community, the self-styled "Jewel of the San Joaquin," is located northwest of Fresno. Its namesake, Andrew Firebaugh (1823-1875), was born in Virginia, but as a young man moved to Texas where he served with that state's Mounted Riflemen in the Mexican War. As with so many of his contemporaries, the Gold Rush drew him to California, where he fought in the Mariposa Indian War under Major James D. Salvage on the expedition that discovered Yosemite. In 1854 he set up a trading post and ferry on the San Joaquin River, "Firebaugh's Ferry," that became a station on the important Butterfield Overland Stage Route. He is credited with constructing the first road over Pacheco Pass.

FITZGERALD MARINE RESERVE
James V. Fitzgerald (1919-2006) was a San Mateo County

Supervisor (1960-80) and ardent conservationist who helped develop thousand of acres of parkland. In 1969 the Board, led by Fitzgerald, passed a bill officially designating the 32-acre Moss Beach tidepool area as a Reserve.

Frank P. Flint

FLINTRIDGE

Frank Putnam Flint (1862-1929) had been a lawyer, a judge, a deputy marshal, a banker a real estate tycoon, and a United States Senator. He and his brother Motley were two of the most prominent leaders in turn-of-the-twentieth-century California. They had moved to the Los Angeles area just in time for the Land Boom--and earned themselves a fortune. Motley became a backer of the nascent film industry and in 1920 rescued Warner Brothers from bankruptcy. Frank was not elected to the U.S. Senate but appointed by the state legislature in 1905. His ties to the First National Bank made him an ideal choice to protect the interests of the Southern Pacific Railroad. Fearing that he would not be re-elected, he decided not to run when his term expired in 1912. About that time he became fixated on developing a suburb for Pasadena and naming it after himself. He bought 1700 acres of *Rancho La Cañada* and named it "Flintridge." By 1916 he had sold only a few of the estate-sized lots, so he started a more forceful campaign to attract prospective purchasers. He built the Flintridge Equestrian Center to go with his Flintridge Bridal Paths, the Flintridge Country Club and—

as the centerpiece--the Flintridge Hotel.

During this time, Motley was caught up in a scandal--the "Million Dollar Pool"--in which tens of thousands of investors were bilked out of $150 million. Frank was counsel for the deal. Motley was indicted for embezzlement, securities violations and conspiracy, but was so well connected the charges were dropped, though Motley fled to France. The prosecutors who dismissed the charges were themselves moved--to San Quentin. In 1931, Motley returned to Los Angeles to face new charges. While in the court house testifying, an enraged investor shot him. Frank was never charged in the deal, but his reputation was destroyed. His reversal of fortune led to a nervous breakdown. He went on an ocean cruise to "settle his nerves" and suffered a fatal heart attack.

In 1976 the community of Flintridge melded with La Cañada to incorporate as La Cañada Flintridge—and gained the distinction of having the longest name of any city in California.

FOLSOM

The New Hampshire-born Joseph Libby Folsom (1817-1855) was an 1840 graduate of West Point. As a captain of the U.S. Army quartermaster department, he arrived in California in 1847 with the Stevenson Regiment. After the Mexican War, he remained in San Francisco where he became Collector of the Port. By 1855, Folsom's health as well as his cash had begun to give out. He hired Theodore Judah to survey and lay out a town site near the mining camp of Negro Bar to be called Granite City. There had been talk since 1852 of a railroad, the first in the West, to be built from Sacramento at least as far as Negro Bar. In February 1855, Folsom accepted the post of president of the fledgling railroad, but died later that year at the age of thirty-eight, too soon to see the development of what was to become the town of Folsom. Only three weeks after his death, the first rail was laid on the new Sacramento Valley Railroad; and the first train completed the trip to Folsom in February, 1856. In the same month, town lots in Granite City, which was renamed Folsom in his honor, were auctioned off, with most of the 2,048 lots sold the first day.

Folsom Lake State Recreation Area and **Folsom Powerhouse State Historic Park** are both near Folsom.

FOSTER CITY

T. Jack Foster, (1902-1968) was born in Mineral Wells, Texas, the youngest of eleven children. He went to law school in Oklahoma and served as city attorney and mayor of Norman, Oklahoma. An entrepreneur by nature, he began constructing residential developments in California, Texas, New Mexico, Kansas, and Hawaii. In 1958 he purchased what was then Brewer's Island, 2,600 acre of nondescript reclaimed marshland of the San Francisco Bay, for $12 million from the Leslie Salt Company, with the idea of creating an entire city. Ground was broken in 1961. Foster died in 1968, convinced of the ultimate success of his great venture. His sons continued the development with large sales of land to other builders and developers. Finally, in 1970, they sold the remaining vacant land, both developed and undeveloped, to Centex West, which completed the project.

FOWLER

The San Joaquin Valley town was named for Thomas Fowler (1829-1884). Born in Belfast, he left Ireland at eighteen, finding work in New York, then working his way across the country before finally settling in the early 1850s in the Visalia area. He saw opportunity not in gold mining but in selling beef to the mining communities. Over time his business prospered until he was the dominant beef supplier in Central California and Nevada, acquiring a 40,000-acre ranch and a cattle herd numbering in the tens of thousands. A railroad switch was built on his ranch, ("Fowler's Switch") around which the town developed. Turning to politics he ran successfully for the State Senate in 1869, staying for several terms. He next turned to mining, which proved a failure, losing him most of his fortune. He died from an accident when he was fifty-five, leaving little money behind, but a good reputation.

FRANKS TRACT

Franks Tract is the largest lake in the Sacramento-San Joaquin Delta. About 3500 acres in size, it was farmland owned by Fred Franks until its levee broke in 1935. Franks brought in a dredger to get the water out, but reclamation was not possible. However, he was able to reclaim the northwest corner that is now called **Little Franks Tract**. Often referred to as a "submerged lake," it now is part of the **Franks Tract State Recreation Area** and is only accessible by boat.

FRAZIER PARK

The Kern County community was named in 1926 for nearby **Frazier Mountain**, which was named in honor of Warren Frazier (1846-1920). He had come west from his home in Missouri to work on the building of the railroad in 1862 and settled in Bakersfield. He and his brothers discovered gold on the mountain while hunting there in 1870. The Frazier mine produced $1 million in gold ore during the 1870s. In 1876 Frazier became the first man through the Kern River gorge.

John C. Frémont

FREMONT

The Fremont area was first settled with the establishment of the Mission San Jose by the Spanish. In the mid-1840's, John C. Frémont (1813-1890) mapped a trail through

Mission Pass to provide access for American settlers into the southeastern San Francisco Bay Area. In 1853,Washington Township was established, taking in the communities of Mission San Jose, Centerville, Niles, Irvington, and Warm Springs. In 1956, they joined together to incorporate as the City of Fremont.

Frémont had been commissioned 2nd lieutenant in the U. S. Topographical Engineers in 1838, while engaged in exploring the country between the Missouri and the northern frontier, and in early in 1843 started with a party of 39 men, and, after a journey of 1,700 miles, reached Great Salt Lake. He then proceeded to the tributaries of the Columbia River and in November started upon the return trip, but, finding himself confronted with danger of death from cold and starvation, turned west and succeeded in crossing the Sierra Nevada range and in March reached Sutter's fort in California. His return journey was conducted safely by the southern route, and he reached Kansas in July 1844

He went on another expedition in 1845, spending the summer along the continental divide and crossing the Sierra again in the winter. Upon refusal of the Mexican authorities to allow him to continue his explorations, he fortified himself with his little force of sixty-four men on a small mountain about thirty miles from Monterey, but when the Mexicans prepared to besiege the place he retreated to Oregon. He was overtaken near Klamath Lake, May 9, 1846, by a courier with dispatches from Washington, directing him to watch over the interests of the United States in the territory, there being reason to fear interference from both Great Britain and Mexico. He promptly returned to California, where the settlers, learning that General Castro was already marching against the settlements, flocked to his camp, and in less than a month Northern California was freed from Mexican authority. He received a lieutenant-colonel's commission and was elected governor of the territory by the settlers.. Near the end of the year General Kearny arrived with a force of dragoons and said that he had orders also to establish a government. Friction between the two rival officers ensued, and Frémont prepared continue as governor in spite of Kearny's orders. For this he was tried by court-martial in Washington, and, after a trial which lasted more than a year, was convicted, January 31, 1847 of "mutiny," "disobedience to the lawful command of a superior officer," and "conduct to the prejudice of good order and military discipline," and was sentenced to dismissal from the service. President Polk approved of the conviction for disobedience and mutiny, but remitted the penalty and Frémont resigned.

In 1848, he started on an independent exploring expedition with a party of thirty-three men, and reached Sacramento in the spring of 1849. He represented California in the United States senate from September, 1850, to March, 1851, and in 1853 made his fifth and last exploring expedition, crossing the Rocky mountains by the route which he had attempted to follow in 1848.

Fremont Peak State Park is near San Juan Bautista.

FRIANT

The Fresno County town had its start as a ferry crossing on the San Joaquin River. In 1856 a ferry license was issued to one C. P. Convers and the location was called Convers Ferry. Over time it was called Hamptonville and Pollasky until 1907 when it took its present name, after Thomas Friant (1840-1927), co-owner of the White-Friant Lumber Company. He and his partner, T. Stewart White, had started the company in Michigan and had diverse lumber operations throughout the country.

FULLERTON

On a duck hunting vacation to the Westminster marshes near Anaheim in what is now Orange County in early 1887, brothers George and Edward Ameriges heard that the California Central Railroad, a subsidiary of the Santa Fe, was looking for land. George H. Fullerton (1853-1929), president of the Pacific Land and Improvement Co., also a Santa Fe subsidiary, had been sent west specifically to purchase land for railroad rights-of-way. The Ameriges learned that a likely site for a town was located north of Anaheim. They began negotiating for the land, arranging to buy 430 acres at a cost of approximately $68,000. They offered free right-of-way and half interest in the land if the railroad survey were altered to include the proposed town site. With George Fullerton's assurance that the area would be included, the Ameriges made the purchase. On July 5, 1887, Edward Amerige drove a stake into a mustard field and the town site was born. The appreciative community voted to name the town in honor of its benefactor, George Fullerton. Or so goes the revised history. According to some, however, it was not a simple, unsolicited "appreciation." Rather, it was part of a deal: the Ameriges would give him an interest in the site and name the new town after Fullerton if he would lay Santa Fe's track across their land.

FUNSTON, FORT

In 1917 the former Lake Merced military reservation in San Francisco was renamed for Frederick Funston (1865-1917). The five-feet-four and slightly built Funston went from a Kansas farm to a life of amazing adventure. Youthful exploring expeditions in this country were followed by two years in the Arctic from which he returned down the Yukon river 1,500 miles by canoe. After ventures in Latin America, he served 18 months with Cuban insurgents, fighting in 22 engagements and reaching the rank of lieutenant-colonel. Invalided home shortly before the Spanish-American War, Funston was made colonel of the 20th Kansas infantry. In 1901 he planned and executed the capture of Aguinaldo, commander of the Filipino army. He received a Congressional Medal of Honor and at 35 was made a brigadier general in the regular army. In 1914, during intervention in Mexico, he commanded Vera Cruz as military governor and was that year made a major general. He is buried in the San Francisco National Cemetery at the Presidio. He had two California connections. In 1891 he served a botanist in a surveying expedition of Death Valley. In 1906 he commanded the Presidio base in San Francisco when the earthquake shook the city. He took control of the city under martial law, and directed the dynamiting of buildings to create fire-breaks to stop the fiery conflagrations that were getting out-of-control.

G

GABRIEL, SAN

The name of the city, the valley and the mountain range stem from the *Misión San Gabriel Arcángel*, the fourth California mission. As the original and oldest settlement north of San Diego and south of San Luis Obispo, it is from San Gabriel that the City of Los Angeles and the greater metropolitan area were established. Saint Gabriel was one of the three archangels mentioned in the Bible

GALT

The history of the small city about twenty miles south of the state capital began during the Gold Rush days of the Sacramento Valley. In 1850 a group of farmers settled around the banks of a small stream, Dry Creek, with plans to grow beef and dairy products. In 1869 the town of Galt was laid out by the Western Pacific Railroad Company. The name was given at the request of John McFarland, a local rancher, in honor of his home town in Ontario, Canada, which in turn was named for the prolific Scottish novelist and Commissioner of the Canada Company, John Galt (1779-1839), who served as Secretary of the Canada

Company from 1824 to 1829, and was charged with assisting the colonization of Upper Canada.

GARBERVILLE

Jacob C. Garber (1824-1904), one of the area's earliest settlers, is often called the "pioneer of pioneers." He was born in Virginia, raised there and in Ohio, where he received his education. In 1845 he came to California, locating in Trinity County, where he engaged in mining for a number of years, later serving as County Recorder. He finally moved to Humboldt County, where he opened a general store and acted as postmaster. When he moved there the town was known as "Dogville." He later named it after himself. In 1887 he relocated to Grangeville, Idaho, and soon was made its postmaster, which position he held until his death.

GARDINER, MT

Located in the center of the Sequoia-Kings Canyon National Park, the 12,908-foot mountain was named by the Whitney Survey party for James T. Gardiner (1842-1912) of which he was a member in the 1860s. He had gone to the famous Sheffield Scientific School at Yale with his boyhood friend Clarence King who he accompanied across the plains in 1863. After surveying in the west, he returned to New York, where he became director of the State Survey for ten years, then entered private practice as a civil engineer.

GEORGETOWN

Lying between the South and Middle Forks of the American River in El Dorado county, the mining town, originally known as Growlersburg, was changed in 1852 to Georgetown. There is some question as to whether it was named for George Ehrenhaft or George Phipps. The former is credited with its founding in 1849; the latter was a leader of a party of seamen-turned-prospectors who arrived on the scene later the same year.

GILROY

Juan Bautista Gilroy (1794-1869) is considered to have been the first English-speaking resident of California. Born John Cameron at Inverness, Scotland, he left home at nineteen as a sailor on a merchant ship bound for an outpost on the Columbia River. He jumped ship at Monterey and, afraid of being tracked down, took his mother's maiden name of Gilroy. In order to remain in California he became a citizen by swearing his allegiance to Spain and being baptized as "Juan Bautista Gilroy." He soon hiked to the southern part of the Santa Clara Valley to a Spanish settlement known as *Rancho San Ysidro*, owned by José Ortega, who as the scout of the Portolá expedition of 1769, was the first European to settle there. Gilroy married Ortega's sister in 1821, became an important member of the community and served as the *alcalde*. He was described as having a weakness for gambling and drinking, and as his debts rose, more and more of his wife's land and possessions were sold to pay them off. The story goes that he died in poverty. In 1867, when the community petitioned for incorporation as a city, it changed the name of San Ysidro to Gilroy to honor the pioneer.

GLENDORA

Nestled beneath the San Gabriel Mountains, modern Glendora was founded in 1887 by George D. Whitcomb (1834-1914) who moved to California from Illinois in the early 1880s. He was the founder of the Whitcomb Locomotive Works in Chicago and Rochelle, Illinois. He purchased several hundred acres of what was called *Rancho San José*, which included the land of present day Pomona, Claremont, La Verne, San Dimas, and Glendora. He built a 26-room estate and then formed the Glendora Land Company to develop the new town. He came up with the name "Glendora" by combining the nickname of his wife, Leadora Bennett Whitcomb {"Dora"), with the location of his home in a "glen" of the San Gabriel Mountains.

GLEN ELLEN

In 1859 Charles V. Stuart (1819-1880) bought a section of a Sonoma County land grant called *Rancho Agua Caliente*, where he would build a house and a thousand-acre vineyard. The latter he named Glen Ellen after his wife, Ellen Stuart. A town grew up around it which also was called Glen Ellen. At her husband's death, Ellen Stuart took over management of the estate, making her one of the first women wine makers in California.

Hugh J. Glenn

GLENN COUNTY

Dr. Hugh J. Glenn (1824-1883) was a Missouri physician who came to California in 1849 and worked for a spell on a gold claim at Murderer's Bar on the American River. He made several journeys overland to bring herds of horses, mules, and cattle from Missouri, before settling permanently in California. In 1867, after a few years farming in Yolo County, he bought some land in what is now Glenn County, but then was part of Colusa County. He began a large-scale wheat-growing operation, buying large tracts of land in *Rancho Jacinto*, eventually owning 45,000 acres, yielding a million bushels, making him the biggest wheat grower in the western world, and his reputation as the world's "Wheat King." Glenn made an unsuccessful bid for the California governorship in 1879. He did not live to see the county named for him as he was shot to death on his own property by an employee.

The county was formed by legislative act in 1891 and named for Glenn, whose estate gave financial backing to a proposal for creating and naming the new county.

GODDARD, MT.
The Whitney survey named the 13,568-foot peak for civil engineer and map-maker George Henry Goddard, (1817-1906) who came to California in 1850 and settled in Sacramento. He prospected for gold but earned a living as an artist, selling sketches of California scenes. With Edgar Mills, he helped found the mining camp of Columbia in Tuolumne County. He laid out the first railroad line in California, the Western Pacific, extending out of Sacramento. In 1861 he became a land examiner for various banks in Sacramento. He assembled a large collection of minerals from California mines and more than 1000 sketches of places he had surveyed. This collection was destroyed in the San Francisco earthquake and fire of 1906.

GOETHE, MT.
Several miles north or Mt. Goddard, the 13,264-foot peak was named in 1949 for the German writer Johannes Wilhelm Goethe (1749-1832) in commemoration of the bicentennial of his birth.

GONZALES
It was founded in 1874 by Mariano (b. 1848) and Alfredo Gonzalez (b. 1845), sons of Teodoro Gonzalez (b. 1806), who arrived in Monterey from Mexico in 1825, where he worked as a sea otter hunter. He served as *alcalde* of Monterey in 1836. He was granted *Rancho Rincon de la Puente del Monte*, consisting of more than 15,000 acres and encompassing present-day Gonzales. Mariano went to Santa Clara College (now University) and Cooper Medical College (now University of California, San Francisco). He and his brother planned the town in 1874 on their father's land. The family spelled their name Gonzalez, but the town uses a final "s" in its spelling.

GORGONIO, MOUNT SAN

The highest mountain in Southern California at 11,503 feet is part of the San Bernardino Mountains. It was named for Saint Gorgonius (2??-304), martyred during the persecution of Christians by the Roman emperor Diocletian. The name is derived from a holding of Mission San Gabriel (1824), later to become *Rancho San Jacinto y San Gorgonio*, a Mexican land grant. Most likely it was founded on or near the Feast Day of the saint, September 9.

San Gorgonio Pass and **San Gorgonio Wilderness** take their names from the peak.

GORMAN

Located in the Tejon Pass north of Los Angeles along the Interstate 5 corridor, the tiny community is named for James Gorman, Sr. (18??-1876) who bought the property, then a stagecoach rest stop, around 1868. A veteran of the Mexican-American War of 1848, he was at Fort Tejon as a teamster in 1854 during its construction.

GREGORIO, SAN

Rancho San Gregorio, consisting of 17,752 acres along the San Mateo coastline, was granted to Antonio Buena in 1839. George Washington Tully Carter in 1865 bought five acres on the bank of **San Gregorio Creek** near the stage road. The following year he advertised the opening of his San Gregorio House as a "summer resort for the citizens of San Francisco." Confident that San Gregorio would be a town one day, Carter stuck it out for three years, long enough to see it develop from a mere stage stop to a busy hamlet. Its namesake, Gregory the Great (540-604), the son of a Roman senator, became a monk at the age of thirty-five, and pope at fifty. He is one of the four Doctors of the Roman Catholic church.

GRIDLEY.

George W. Gridley (1818-1880), a native New Yorker who had moved to Illinois to raise sheep and cattle, came west in 1850, driving a herd of livestock across the plains. He lost the herd on that journey, but found the area that would become Gridley an ideal place to settle. He then returned to Illinois and this time successfully brought back a herd of sheep. He soon established a ranch of almost a thousand acres and raised a family of ten children. Over time he became one of the leading wool growers and grain farmers in Butte County. In 1870 Gridley convinced the California and Oregon Railroad Company to build a side track he could use to load his wool and grain on to rail cars for shipment to market. The "switch at Gridley's Station" became the town of Gridley.

GRIFFITH PARK

The Los Angeles park was once a part of a Spanish settlement known as *Rancho Los Felis*. The Governor of *Alta California* granted it to Corporal Vincente Felis in the 1770s. The land stayed in his family for over a century, being subdivided through generations, until Griffith J. Griffith (1850-1919), a wealthy mining speculator, purchased what remained of the *rancho* in 1882. He was born in Wales and came to America as a teenager. He worked as a journalist and mining advisor before making his fortune in Mexican silver mines and, subsequently, southern California real estate. He moved to Los Angeles after purchasing the *rancho* and spent the rest of his life there. Griffith enjoyed being referred to as "Colonel Griffith" though it seems he was never officially commissioned as an officer (nor is it clear that he even served in the military). During a trip abroad, Griffith had discovered the great public parks of Europe and decided that Los Angeles, needed a "Great Park" for the public in order to become a great city. In December, 1896, he donated 3,015 acres of *Rancho Los Felis* to the City of Los Angeles in order to create a park in his name. It became the largest urban park in the U.S. with wilderness areas and included a central peak that he named Griffith Peak. But on September 3, 1903, Griffith shot his wife during a dispute in a Santa Monica hotel, for which he was imprisoned in San Quentin for three years for attempted murder. Because of this affair, petitioners were successful in renaming Griffith Peak "Mount Hollywood."

Inspired by Mount Wilson Observatory, in 1912 Griffith J. Griffith offered the city of Los Angeles a gift of $100,000 for an observatory to be built atop of Mount Hollywood. but the city refused the offer and responded, in part "On behalf of the rising generation of girls and boys, we protest against the acceptance of this bribe. . . . This community is neither so poor nor so lost to sense of public decency that it can afford to accept this money." However several years after his death the city did accept the offer and the Griffith Observatory was built.

GRIMES
The little village on Grand Island in Colusa County is named for Cleaton Grimes, who located there in 1851, building a cabin on the riverbank, where he won the distinction of introducing hog-raising to the county, though he spent no little of his time keeping the bears from devouring his stock.

GROVER BEACH
The parents of D(wight) W(illiam) Grover (1853-1924) came to California from Maine hoping to find gold, but instead eventually landed in Santa Cruz where his father made his fortune in lumber, and where D. W. was born. In 1887 he left Santa Cruz for Pizmo Beach with plans to develop a community. He filed plans at the San Luis Obispo County Court House and founded what would become Grover City. Its name was officially changed to Grover Beach in 1992.

GUERNEVILLE
In 1860 R.B. Lundsford established a lumber camp on the north bank of the Russian River which grew with success and became known as "Stumptown." In 1867 a 25-year-old Swiss immigrant, George E. Guerne (1841-1921), arrived in the area, purchased land, and laid out a subdivision which he dubbed 'Guernewood Park." He also built and operated a sawmill in Stumptown, which was soon renamed Guerneville in honor of its most important citizen.

GUSTINE

The Merced County town was established in the early 1900s as a station on the Southern Pacific railroad and named after Augustine "Gussie" Miller (1871-1879), who had been killed by a runaway horse when she was eight. She was the daughter of Henry Miller (1827-1916), the "Cattle King," an early California land baron and agricultural pioneer. The German-born, one-time butcher, through his Miller & Lux Corporation, owned outright some 1,400,000 acres and had under his control through lease and grazing arrangements ten times that much--a domain of about 22,000 square miles in all, spread over California, Oregon, and Nevada.

H

HAHN STATE RECREATION AREA, KENNETH

Kenneth Hahn (1920-1997) served on the Los Angeles County Board of Supervisors for forty years (1952-1992) and was instrumental in convincing the government to use the land which constitutes the park as a recreation area.. When the park opened it was called the Baldwin Hills State Recreation Area, but was renamed in the Supervisor's honor in 1988.

HAIGHT, THE

The San Francisco neighborhood (also known as "Upper Haight" or "Haight-Ashbury") is named for its main thoroughfare, Haight Street, which honors Henry Haight (1820-1869), a New York-born banker and, later, philanthropist, who moved to San Francisco in 1850 to serve as manager of the bank Page, Bacon & Co.

HAMILTON ARMY AIRFIELD DISCONTIGUOUS HISTORIC DISTRICT

Hamilton Army Airfield in Novato was built in 1932 as a bombardment base for the Army Air Corps and named for pilot First Lieutenant Lloyd Andrew Hamilton, originally from Marin County, killed in World War I. In August. 1918, he received the Distinguished Service Cross for heroism after leading a bombing attack on a German airfield behind enemy lines. He died in action two weeks later. The base was deactivated in 1989, most of it being transferred to the city of Novato. **Hamilton Field** is now a residential community.

HAMILTON CITY

The small community along the Sacramento River in Glenn County was founded by a beet sugar company in 1905 as the site for a processing plant and named for J. G. Hamilton, its president at the time and promoter of the town. Described in one contemporary report as "a New York capitalist," Hamilton had been involved with the Oxnard brothers in several earlier sugar ventures around the country.

HAMILTON, MOUNT

In 1861 William H. Brewer, then director of field work for the California State Geological Survey, invited his friend Reverend Laurentine Hamilton (1826-1882) to accompany him on a mountain-climbing expedition. Their goal was a peak judged to be the highest in the Diablo Range, thirteen miles east of San Jose. After an arduous mule ride, the party hiked the last three miles on foot. "As we neared the summit," Brewer later recalled, "Mr. Hamilton pushed on ahead of us, and reaching it, swung his hat in the air and shouted back to us: 'First on top - for this is the highest point.' " Sometime later that year, it was suggested that the mountain be called Hamilton. It is the site of the Lick Observatory.

Hamilton, born in New York where he also trained fro the Presbyterian ministry, came to California in 1865 where, after two postings elsewhere, was sent to Oakland in 1865. He became estranged from the Presbyterian Church and established the Independent Church where on Easter Sunday morning, 1882, just as he had said "We know not what matter is . . ." he dropped in his pulpit and died.

HANFORD

Like so many other young men, James Madison Hanford (1827-1911) came to California from his native New York in search of adventure and wealth. For twenty years he worked at various occupations--hardware store owner, justice of the peace, school teacher—before finding employment with the Central Pacific Railroad as Special Assistant to the President. The railroad later became the Southern Pacific and Hanford became its Paymaster. During the mid-nineteenth century the railroad grew quickly, with employees scattered over a huge area. At that time paper money was heavily discounted so that wages had to be paid in silver and gold coins. A specially remodeled Pullman car was used to pay out wages to workers. In the 1870's, with only one such car, it took two months to pay all employees. Three pay cars were outfitted in 1888, and the railroad began paying wages monthly.. The pay cars were heavily guarded, their schedules kept secret and they did not run at night. Hanford's trustworthiness as Paymaster was appreciated by the railroad; its president gave Hanford the opportunity to select a town site on the Goshen-Alcalde branch when it was being built and named it in his honor. In January, 1877, Hanford (a former sheep camp) was placed on the map by the sale of sixty-eight business lots fronting on the railroad which had come through the previous October Hanford retired from the Southern Pacific in 1908 after thirty-nine years with the railroad.

HARBIN SPRINGS

James M. Harbin came from Missouri to the Napa area in 1846 and, with Archibald Ritchie, discovered the hot springs in 1852. Harbin bought out his partner in 1860 and built a home and a resort that by 1909 had accommodations for 200 guests.

HATFIELD STATE RECREATION AREA, GEORGE

The park, near Turlock in Merced County, opened in 1953 and honors George Juan Hatfield (1887-1953). He attended Stanford Law School before practicing in San Francisco. He served as U.S. Attorney for the state's Northern District (1925-1933) and Lieutenant Governor (1935-1939). His wife's maternal grandfather, Colonel James J. Stevinson, fought in the Mexican War and was an early settler of Merced County.

HAWTHORNE

The city's namesake is the author Nathanial Hawthorne (1804-1864). He was not its founder; in fact, the New England novelist never set foot in California. The city, on what was once barley fields, was developed in 1905 by Benjamin I. Harding and Harry Dana Lombard. The name of their corporation--Hawthorne Development Company-- was selected by Harding's daughter, Laurine Harding Woolwine, who shared her birthday with the famous writer.

HAYWARD

William Hayward (1815-1891) had been working at a shoe factory in Georgetown, Massachusetts when he heard of the discovery of gold in California; he promptly booked passage on a steamer to San Francisco. Upon his arrival, Hayward saw that making shoes would be more profitable than mining gold. He squatted on Guillermo Castro's ranch in the East Bay. Castro tried to evict him, but Hayward persuaded him otherwise by making him a pair of boots. His stubbornness and shoe-making ability convinced Castro to hire him. Hayward set up a small store and saved up enough money to buy forty acres of Castro's land, including what is now the downtown Hayward area. On this land he set up a store and a small dairy. Castro immigrated to Chile with most of his family in 1864, after he lost his land in a card game. His ranch was split up and sold to various locals, Hayward among them. He constructed a resort hotel which eventually grew to a hundred rooms. The surrounding area came to be called "Haywards" after the hotel which bore the name "Haywards Hotel" (no apostrophe before the "s"). Hayward also served a couple of terms on the Alameda County Board of Supervisors. In 1876, the town was chartered under the name of "Haywards." However, it was not legal to name a post office after a living person, so the official name was "Haywood." In 1876, "Haywood" was incorporated as the "Town of Haywards," with a population of 1,100. In 1894, the "s" in "Haywards" was dropped and in 1928 the city's name was changed to the "City of Hayward."

HEALDSBURG

When the 25-year-old Harmon G. Heald (1824-1858) heard of the Gold Rush, he and two friends left Missouri and headed overland with four yoke of oxen, a wagon and two saddle horses. Heald settled in Sonoma County, where he squatted on some land by the main road to the counties to the north and opened up a store. He then laid out a grid for a town which he named for himself, and sold lots for $15 each. In a short time the town grew. Heald was elected to the California State Assembly (1856-57). Unfortunately, he died the following year at the age of thirty-four.

William Randolph Hearst

HEARST MEMORIAL STATE BEACH, W. R.

In 1953 the Hearst Corporation donated the area comprising the W. R. Hearst Memorial Beach to San Luis Obispo County in memory of William Randolph Hearst (1863-1951). It was later transferred to the State to complement the operation of the adjacent **Hearst San Simeon State Historical Monument** and **Hearst San Simeon State Park**. The newspaper owner who built up the country's largest newspaper chain was the only son of George Hearst, a gold-mine owner and U. S. Senator from California (1886-1891). A larger-than- life figure, W.R. Hearst was a journalist, publisher, builder, art collector, and politician. His California connection is most dramatically illustrated by the fabulous estate he built at San Simeon, popularly known as "Hearst's Castle.

HEBER

The Imperial County town was established in 1903 by the California Development Company and named in honor of its president, Anthony H. Heber, who had been brought from Chicago by Charles R. Rockwood, to assist him in promoting the irrigation of the Colorado Desert.

HELENA, MOUNT SAINT

Originally known by its Indian name of Mount Mayacamas, it was changed after Russian scientists hiked to the summit in 1841 and left a plaque inscribed with the date and, according to legend, the name of Princess Helena de Gagarin, the wife of the then commander of Fort Ross, Count Alexander G. Rotchev, and a godchild of the Czar. Some accounts say that she was among the hiking party and named it for her patron saint and that of the Empress of Russia. This "creation myth" has been no doubt romanticized. Gudde mentions that the Empress' name was Alexandra, not Helena. and that while it is possible that the Russians did name the mountain there is no record of it. He believed that as one of the Russian ships was named *Saint Helena* and the peak was visible from offshore, that "the naming from aboard ship would be more likely than the christening by a princess." Saint

Helena (c. 250-330), the mother of Constantine the Great, is best known as the legendary discoverer, at Golgotha, of the "True Cross" on which Christ had been crucified.

HENDY WOODS STATE PARK

The redwood groves, and the park which was constructed around them, in Mendocino County's Anderson Valley are named for Joshua P. Hendy (1822-1891) who, in the late 1800's, claimed the area as his own. Born in England, Hendy came to California in 1849, but he didn't mine for gold. Taking a practical line, he recognized that building materials were in short supply, so he built a redwood lumber mill, the first in California. In 1856 he started the Joshua Hendy Iron Works in San Francisco to manufacture mining equipment; it would become a world leader in mining technology. In 1958 the then owner of the property, the Masonite Corporation, joined with the Save-the-Redwoods League in donating 405 acres to the state parks system.

HERCULES

The California Powder Works plants made black powder, an explosive substance used mostly in guns. It opened a plant near Golden Gate Park in 1869. With the growing population of San Francisco and the explosive nature of their product, the company was forced to find a less populous location. A site in Contra Costa County was found and a dynamite manufacturing plant was opened. The company sold its dynamite under the "Hercules Powder" brand. The Greek mythological hero's name was chosen to showcase its potency. When the town became incorporated in 1900, the name Hercules became a natural choice for the community leaders, who were also the plant managers.

HILLSBOROUGH

The San Mateo County city is indirectly named for a man. It was part of the Mexican land grant *Rancho San Mateo* purchased in 1846 by William Davis Merry Howard, son of a Hillsboro, New Hampshire shipping magnate. Howard settled his family in this area, which attracted wealthy San Franciscans, and named it after his paternal home. In 1910 Hillsborough residents voted to incorporate. The New Hampshire town was named for Sir Willis Hill (1718-1793), Earl of Hillsborough, an English noble who served as Secretary of State for the American Colonies for several years prior to the Declaration of Independence.

HOLLISTER

The largest community in San Benito County was named for Colonel W. W. Hollister (1818-1886), one of the first men to bring improved sheep stock to California. A native of Ohio, he dropped out of Kenyon College to pursue farming until he was thirty-three, when he sold everything, bought a few hundred head of livestock and set off to California, where he sold them and returned home. The following year, 1853, he drove a flock of 9,000 head of Merino sheep and 200 cattle, 50 helpers and 11 covered wagons. across the plains. The trek took almost a year-and-a-half to complete. He used to say that every one of those sheep earned him a thousand dollars before he died. In the course of twenty or thirty years he became a millionaire, the owner of over a hundred thousand acres of land and one of the largest sheep owners in the state. He took the stock north, and went into the business of breeding improved sheep on an extensive scale. Eventually, with others, he bought the San Justo ranch in the San Benito Valley, then a portion of Monterey County. Although a large land-holder himself, Colonel Hollister was a pioneer in breaking up the large holdings to facilitate settlement. The San Justo ranch was subdivided and sold to a colony of settlers for some $25,000 less than was offered by a speculator.

In 1868 at the first town meeting of the Rancho San Justo Homestead Association of farmers, a dispute arose over the town's name. It was suggested that it be called San Justo. However, one person protested so strongly against adding one more name to the growing list of saints' names in California, that San Justo was rejected. The name of "Hollister" was agreed upon instead and incorporation took place four years later. Soon after the sale of the San Justo ranch, Hollister bought land in Santa Barbara, to which, until the time of his death, he gave most of his time and attention.

HOLTVILLE

The self-proclaimed "Carrot Capital of the World" was started by William Franklin Holt (1868-1922), the founding entrepreneur of Imperial Valley. He was a banker from Missouri who had first migrated west to Colorado when he was thirty-two where he worked for a few years with a manufacturing company before moving to Arizona to open a bank. In 1900 he sold his interests and moved to Redlands, California. In 1901 he paid a visit to Imperial Valley where saw its agricultural possibilities and the necessity for a railroad and undertook the building of the first line to the valley. He would control the locally based California Development Company that controlled the water. In the process he was the first to think of building a town east of the Alamo River. In 1903 Holtville was born. Its name was originally Holton; however it was changed to its present name at the request of the Postal Service because the former name sounded too much like Colton. By 1910, when Harold Bell Wright was writing his popular novel, *The Winning of Barbara Worth*, he used his friend Holt as the prototype of Barbara Worth's father, a paragon of responsible local capitalism.

HUGHSON

Located in the heart of the Central Valley in Stanislaus County, it was founded as a township in 1907. Prior to that, it consisted of the wheat fields owned by Hiram Hughson (1838-1911), who had come to California by steamer in 1861 from New York with only seventy-five cents to his name. He eventually took up farming in Stockton, where he lost an arm in an accident, though it did not stop him from working the land. In 1882 he bought 1000 acres south of the Tuolumne River and eventually added 5000 more where he raised wheat. The San Joaquin Railroad purchased land from Hughson for their tracks, and the station became known as the "Hughson Stop." The town came about because Hughson, at age 61, did not want to make the changes necessary to accommodate irrigation. Water started flowing through Turlock Irrigation District canals in 1901, thanks to the construction of the La Grange Dam in 1894. Hughson decided to move to Modesto and placed his land in the hands of the Hughson Town Company which opened it up for settlement. It made him a wealthy man; at his death he was worth over a million dollars.

HUMBOLDT COUNTY

The German explorer and naturalist Alexander von Humboldt (1769-1859) was probably, next to Napoleon, the most famous man in Europe in the early nineteenth century. He traveled extensively in Latin America, but never in North America. The naming of the county for him came about in the spring of 1850, when several shiploads of adventurers arrived from San Francisco. Their expectations were excited by word from a group of explorers that they had located a bay affording access to the inland gold mines just a few hundred miles to the north. The *Laura Virginia* became the first ship in 44 years to sail into the bay. The Laura Virginians selected a stretch of shoreline opposite the mouth of what they promptly named **Humboldt Bay** (in honor of the explorer), as did they the community to be built there. Afterwards they voted to give Baron von Humboldt the choice lot in the city of his name, and a deed to the same was written and sent to him, with a full account of the adventures of the company, for which they received his kind acknowledgement.

Henry E. Huntington

HUNTINGTON BEACH/PARK

Henry E. Huntington (1850-1927) was a nephew of Collis
P. Huntington, one of the Big Four railroad magnates that
created the transcontinental railway system. Henry was
born in Oneonta, New York. When he was twenty-one his
uncle Collis took him with him to inspect a part of the
Chesapeake and Ohio system he was developing. Not long
afterwards Henry accepted an offer from his uncle to
manage a sawmill cutting railroad ties at St. Albans, West
Virginia. From then on his career was fully concerned with
railroads and transportation. He remained at the sawmill
for five years, returned to Oneonta for a time, and then
became superintendent of construction for a portion of
the Chesapeake and Ohio. In 1884 he became
superintendent of construction for the Kentucky Central
Railroad, and two years later was named a receiver of the
road. In 1890, when Collis took over as president of the
Southern Pacific, Henry was called to San Francisco to
serve as assistant to the president. When Collis died in
1900, he left a third of his estate to Henry, who, with the
other heirs, sold control of Southern Pacific to E. H.
Harriman of the Union Pacific. For several years prior to
Collis' death, Henry had become increasingly concerned
with the management of electric street railways, to which
he devoted his time after 1902. Turning his attention to

115

Los Angeles, he began buying transportation lines there, and transferred his headquarters there in 1902. Finding inadequate local service in the Los Angeles area, he connected, consolidated, and then extended the existing lines until, in about ten years, he had created an interurban system surpassing anything of its kind. In addition to this "Orange Empire," as it was called, he organized the Los Angeles railway system, providing service within the city. In 1903 Huntington began collecting rare books and manuscripts. His collection grew into The Huntington Library, which included an art collection and botanical gardens on his estate in San Marino, California.

Huntington Beach, incorporated in 1909, was established by one of Henry's real estate development companies, the Huntington Beach Company, A couple of developers named Burbank and Baker arrived in the area that would be **Huntington Park** in 1899. In two years they controlled a 100-acre tract of land called Sunrise Tract. They subdivided it and changed the name to La Park. In order to entice Huntington to extend a line of his Pacific Electric Railway to and through their development, in 1902 they granted Huntington a right-of-way for his railway and they changed the name to Huntington Park. However, the name La Park stuck and the Post Office did not change the name until the city was incorporated.

HUNTER LIGGETT, FORT

Originally designated Hunter Liggett Military Reservation in 1941, it is named for Lieutenant General Hunter Liggett (1857-1935), commander of the 41st National Guard Division, and, later, the First Corps of the American Expeditionary Forces during World War I. He also served as Chief of Staff for General John Pershing. In 1975 the reservation was re-designated Fort Hunter Liggett Military Installation.. Almost 200,000 acres in area, and situated in Monterey County, it was once the summer ranch of William Randolph Hearst.

I

IGNACIO

Ignacio Pacheco (1808-1864) was born in San Jose, the only child and namesake of its *alcalde*. When he was nineteen he enlisted at the San Francisco Presidio. After his service, he looked for a place where he could graze cattle, selecting some land near Novato (an area that now includes Ignacio, Hamilton Field, and Bel Marin Keys) and built a house there. In 1840 Governor Alvarado granted him official title to *Rancho San José*. Pacheco went on to become a judge and second *alcalde* of San Rafael. At his *rancho* he hunted game, built a hacienda, raised cattle and horses and founded the town named for him.

IRVINE

James Irvine's father, James, Sr., arrived in San Francisco during the Gold Rush to work as a miner and merchant. Capitalizing on a successful produce and grocery business started in 1854, he began investing in real estate, bought half-interests in three major southern California *ranchos* as a silent partner of Flint, Boxby & Co., a sheep-raising venture. In 1878 he acquired his partners' interests for $150,000. His 110,00 acres stretched twenty-three miles from the Pacific Ocean to the Santa Ana River--about a third of present day Orange County. In 1893 his son, James, Jr. (1867-1947), came into full possession of the ranch which he incorporated into The Irvine Company one year later. Taking advantage of the fertility of the land and experimenting with new methods of cultivation, he created a large-scale agribusiness that, by 1910, was recognized as the state's most productive farm.

In 1959 the University of California asked The Irvine Company for a thousand acres for a new campus. It agreed and the State accepted the land and purchased an additional five hundred acres. The Irvine Company planners drew up master plans for a city of 50,000 people surrounding the university. The Irvine Industrial Complex West (now known as The Irvine Business Complex) opened and the villages of Turtle Rock, University Park, Culverdale, the Ranch, and Walnut were completed by 1970. The following year the residents of these communities voted to incorporate a substantially larger city than that envisioned by the original plan in order to control the future of the area and protect its tax base; it would be called "Irvine."

IRWIN, FORT

President Franklin Roosevelt established the thousand square-mile Mojave Anti-Aircraft Range in 1940. Two years later it was renamed Camp Irwin in honor of Major General George LeRoy Irwin (1869-1931), commander of the 57th Field Artillery Brigade during World War I.

IRWINDALE

The San Gabriel Valley city was known as Jardin de Roca, Cactus Town, Jack Rabbit Town and Sonora Town in the latter part of the nineteenth century until a man with the surname of Irwin arrived in 1899. As the story goes, his claim to fame was that he had the area's first gasoline-powered water pump, which allowed him to sink a well so

118

as to cultivate a large enough area to become a successful citrus farmer. Nothing else seems to be known of Mr. Irwin.

ISABELLA, LAKE

The Kern River Valley town of Isabella was founded the year of the 1893 Columbian Exposition (aka the Chicago World's Fair) when the name of Queen Isabella of Spain (1451-1504) was popular. She, of course, was responsible for sending Columbus on his 1492 voyage. A dam on the Kern River was authorized in 1944 and many residents of the Valley were told that their town would be under water when the dam was completed. The town moved south to what had been known as Hot Springs Valley and became the town of Lake Isabella.

J

JACINTO, SAN

In 1774 when the Spanish explorer de Anza passed through this area of what would become known as the Inland Empire, he named it San Jacinto, which translates to St. Hyacinth. It was applied to the valley, the river, and **Mt. San Jacinto**, at 10,804 feet, one of the tallest peaks in southern California. After Spain ceded the area to Mexico, the Estudillo family of San Diego received a land grant in 1842 that included the area. With the coming of settlers in the nineteenth century, the city of San Jacinto bodied forth, incorporating in 1888.

Saint Hyacinth (1185-1257) was a Polish-born Dominican priest who ministered in Eastern and Northern Europe in the early thirteenth century. Sometimes called the "Apostle of the North," he was canonized in 1594.

JACKSON

It is believed that the Amador County seat was founded by a transplanted New Yorker named Colonel Alden A. M.

Jackson (18??-1876) who, it is said, passed through the area in 1848 with a group of prospectors. He moved on to Tuolomne County where the following year he founded the town of **Jacksonville**, now inundated by the waters of Don Pedro Reservoir. In 1850 it was the principal river town in the area and the center for thousands of miners working the rich bed of the Tuolumne River. However this creation story is problematic. Jackson's own website states that it might be named after the Colonel or Andrew Jackson! One historian even avers that it is named for Stonewall Jackson; another that Jackson was a "famous Indian fighter" while yet another that he was a popular local lawyer. It is unlikely that it is named for Alden A. M. Jackson who would have been living in San Francisco at the time and who moved to San Bernardino where he became its first attorney. It is likely that the town's namesake is another "Col. Jackson" altogether, not a lawyer, but a miner-turned-storekeeper.

JAMESTOWN

In June 1848--about the time word was seeping out about the gold find at Sutter's Mill--Benjamin Wood of Clatsop Plains, Oregon, found some sizable chunks of it in a Sierra stream in Tuolumne County that he dubbed "Wood's Creek" and established camp at "Wood's Crossing." The following winter, stories circulated around San Francisco about the discovery. When spring came, hundreds of miners flocked to the area which soon became known as the "Gateway to the Mother Lode." One of those who arrived was Colonel George F. James (1827-1869). He brought a wife, servants, and a wagon full of supplies and treated everyone to champagne. The miners were duly impressed with the Colonel and immediately named the town in his honor (often referred to as Jimtown). Because he had been a lawyer, the locals appointed him as the town magistrate. He also ran a hotel and store and gained some fame after serving as the defense attorney during the first murder trial in Tuolumne Country in 1849. One morning in 1858 the town folk discovered that James had beat a hasty exit during the night. Among his activities, he had been paying script against investments in his mining projects. The scripts far exceeded any proceeds the project would produce. The miners were angry enough to change the town's name to American Camp; however, the post office had been established by the government, so the name remained Jamestown.

JENNER

It is not certain how the Sonoma County coastal hamlet came by its name. The prevailing theory is that is named for one Charles Jenner, who arrived at the mouth of the Russian River about 1868. An aspiring writer seeking a secluded place to work on a book, he obtained permission from the landowner to put up a cabin in the narrow canyon above the meadow. The canyon became known as "Jenner Gulch." When the community grew large enough to become a town and give itself a name, it selected "Jenner by the Sea"—most likely because Jenner Gulch had become a landmark. Just exactly who Jenner was and whether he ever did write that book is not known.

JOAQUIN, SAN

San Joaquin County was one of the original counties created in 1850 at the time of statehood. It takes its name from the **San Joaquin River**. In the early 1800s Lieutenant Gabriel Moraga, commanding an expedition in the lower Central Valley, gave the name of *San Joaquin* to a rivulet that springs from the Sierra Nevada and empties into Buena Vista Lake. That part of the valley became known as **San Joaquin Valley.** *Joaquin* is the Spanish name for Joachim, who, according to Christian tradition, is the father of the Virgin Mary, and the husband of Saint Anne.

JOHNSTONVILLE

The village in Lassen County is named for Robert Johnston (1826-1898), an early pioneer who arrived in the Honey Lake Valley by covered wagon in 1859 and lived there for more than twenty years. It was initially called Toadtown at its founding in 1857, as local legend had it that in the early settlement, whenever a heavy rainstorm came, the ground was covered with little toads. It was changed to Johnstonville in 1864.

JONES, FORT

The Siskiyou County community takes its name from the military post that was established there in 1852 and named for Roger Jones (1780-1852), brevet major-general and the Adjutant General of the Army 1825-52. The fort was garrisoned by Company 3, 4th U.S. Infantry from 1853 until it was abandoned five years later. Jones, a Virginian, had once been an officer of the Marine Corps until his appointment as Adjutant General in 1825, a post he held until his death. Jones seems to have been a colorful figure. In 1830, he was sentenced by a court-martial for issuing orders without authority and saying to the Commanding General of the Army, "I defy you, sir; I defy you!" Notwithstanding, he was permitted to remain Adjutant General for an additional twenty-two years.

JORDAN, MOUNT

The 13,271-foot summit in Tulare County, on the boundary of Kings Canyon and Sequoia National Parks, was named for David Starr Jordan (1851-1931) by the Sierra Club in 1925 and ratified by the U.S. Geographic Board the following year. Jordan had served as president of Indiana University (1885-1891), before holding the same office at Stanford (1891-1913) In August, 1899, Jordan, with a party of Stanford associates, spent several weeks in the Bubbs Creek region of Kings River. On that occasion they explored and mapped Ouzel Creek, to which they gave its name, and climbed Mount Stanford. For a portion of the peak now named Mount Jordan he proposed the name Crag Reflection, but this was never adopted. When notified that it was to be named for him, he wrote "I feel much honored to be associated in any way with these great granite mountains, and also to get in line with my fellow evolutionists, Dana, Lyell, and the rest of them. I am sure that Agassiz would have been one of us if he had been born a little later or could have lived a little longer."

JOSE, SAN

San Jose was founded by Lieutenant José Joaquín Moraga as *El Pueblo de San José de Guadalupe* in November, 1777, as a farming community. It was the first civil settlement in Alta California. It takes its name from Saint Joseph who, according to Christian lore, was the husband of Mary, the mother of Jesus. The second part of its name comes from the nearby Guadalupe River, named by the De Anza Expedition in 1776 *Rio de Nuestra Señora de Guadalupe*, in honor of the Mexican saint who was the principal patron saint of the expedition. The **San Jose Hills** and the city of **South San Jose Hills** in Los Angeles County are also named for St. Joseph.

JOSHUA TREE

The small community is nestled in a segment of the Mojave Desert and is the gateway community to the West Entrance of **Joshua Tree National Park**, an 800,000-acre preserve with groves of Joshua Trees. It is thought that Mormon pioneers, traveling through the area, named the tree after the biblical figure Joshua, because its uplifted limbs reminded them of him praying and waving to the heavens.

JUAN BAUTISTA, SAN

Named for the Mission of that name founded in 1797 in honor of Saint John the Baptist, the San Benito County city was once the largest town in central California and the hub of travel between the northern and central parts of the state. It is also the site of the **San Juan Bautista State Historic Park.**

JUAN CAPISTRANO, SAN

The Orange County city takes its name from the San Juan Capistrano Mission, founded in 1776 by Franciscan missionaries and named for Saint John Capistran (1385-1456), known in his native Italy as Giovanni di Capistrano. He had been a lawyer and governor before joining the Franciscan Order. He would become a theologian, author,

124

preacher, Vatican diplomat, and soldier, leading a wing of the Christian army against the Turks in the Battle of Belgrade.

JUAN, NORTH SAN

The town in Nevada County acquired its name in 1853, when a prospector who had accompanied General Winfield Scott when Scott landed at the Mexican port of Vera Cruz, was mining near the town's present site. He was impressed with the resemblance of a bluff nearby to the castle of San Juan de Ulua, which guards the entrance to the port. He expressed his opinion, and the bluff was dubbed San Juan. Afterward that name was applied to the town. In 1857, when an application to establish a post office there was filed, postal authorities required a different name, as an office had already been established at another town of that name in Monterey County. The resourceful citizens thereupon added the prefix "North" to the name. San Juan de Ulua was named by the Spanish *conquistadores* who arrived there on the feast day of San Juan in 1518. San Juan is "Saint John" and in this case refers to John the Baptist who is said to have baptized Jesus and lost his head to Salome.

Theodore Judah

JUDAH, MOUNT

Theodore Judah (1826-1863) was a civil engineer, lobbyist, rail-roader and surveyor. In 1854 the president of the

125

Sacramento Valley Railroad, asked him to make a survey from Sacramento to Folsom, an enterprise which whet his thirst for constructing a transcontinental railroad. For the next two years Judah lobbied Congress for his plan. In 1860 he was shown a more practical passage through the Sierra instead of Donner's Pass; plans were drawn up and a year later he was able to get backing for a scientific survey. When the Pacific Railroad Act was signed into law on July 1, 1862, he was ready to start work but he became disenchanted with the financial backers. Rancorous arguments followed with the result that Judah left California in October for the East to find new investors. Unfortunately while his ship was crossing the Isthmus of Panama, he came down with Yellow Fever and died a week later in New York. Thus the man who had so ardently pushed for a transcontinental railway did not survive to see it realized. Mount Judah is next to Donner Pass and the rail line runs through it.

JULIAN

Julian was founded after the end of the Civil War when some Confederate veterans from Georgia journeyed west to strike it rich in unsettled country. Among these were cousins Drue Bailey and Michael S. Julian who came upon a meadow between Volcano Mountain and the Cuyamacas. They were there in 1869 when gold was discovered. It was San Diego County's first and only gold rush. Though Bailey actually laid out the town and offered lots free to anyone who would immediately build on them, he named it Julian City for his cousin Mike because, he said—and he was considered a bit of joker--Julian was the handsomest man in the camp. Julian served as County Assessor from 1871 to 1873. He later moved to Long Beach and opened the Julian Hotel.

K

KEELER

The silver-mining boomtown on the eastern shore of Owens Lake is named for Julius M. Keeler (1825-1890) who arrived in Owens Valley in the winter of 1879-80 to represent the Owens Lake Mining and Milling Company, of which he was a major stockholder. He erected a silver-quartz mill and a town grew up around it.

Keeler had been born in New York and attended Union College there. With news of the Gold Rush, he and a group of fellow students purchased an aging ship and sailed for California, arriving in San Francisco. Keeler labored in the mines until 1851 when he moved north to Oregon where he founded Oregon State University and became a faculty member, then the head of the public school of Napa City. When the Civil War began, Keeler returned east, serving as 1st Lieutenant in Colonel Colt's regiment from Hartford, Connecticut. Following the war, he worked as a commission merchant in New York City, with western connections. He returned to California in 1872, continuing in business, and served as supervisor of the Owens Lake Mining and Milling Company.

KELSEYVILLE

The Lake County community was first called "Kelsey Town" in the 1860's in memory of its first settler, Andrew Kelsey, who was believed murdered in 1849 by local Native Americans in revenge for his mistreatment of them while they built his house. In 1850 a troop of soldiers came to punish them for the killing, but they found that they had taken refuge on various islands in Clear Lake. After several battles, a treaty was negotiated. Kelsey and his brother Benjamin had come to California in 1841 with the Bidwell-Bartleson party

KENTFIELD

Albert Emmett Kent (1830-1901), a merchant, banker, and founder of the packing industry in Chicago, came to California in 1871 to improve his poor health and bought land in Marin County from the estate of James Ross where Kent and his wife built a colonial mansion, which he called "Tamalpais," the name which the railroad subsequently applied to the settlement. It later became known as "Kent" and finally, in 1905, "Kentfield."

Kent's son, William, donated 300 acres of land on Mount Tamalpais to the United States Government as a national monument to be known as the Muir Woods.

KERMAN

Located in western Kern County, the town site, first established by the Southern Pacific Railroad Company as a way station with a pump and watering tank in 1891, was originally named Collis in honor of the president of the railroad, Collis P. Huntington. In 1900 Los Angeles developers, William G. Kerckhoff (1856-1929) and Jacob Mansar (1858-c.1920), purchased 3,027 acres of land from the Bank of California and formed the Fresno Irrigated Farms Company. In 1906 Collis was renamed Kerman from the first syllable of the men's surnames. Kerckhoff had come to Los Angeles from Indiana in 1878, going into the lumber business. In 1887 he built the first ocean-going ship in the United States to use oil for fuel. In the 1890s he formed the San Gabriel Power Company, the first concern to use hydroelectric power in Los Angeles. He also invested in natural gas, being an original partner in the Southern California Gas Corporation in 1910. He was also a large-scale land developer, being part of the partnerships which founded Beverly Hills and Del Mar. He lived with his family in a large mansion in Los Angeles which was donated to USC after his death, where it was named Kerckhoff Hall. Shortly before his death he funded a building of the same name at UCLA. He was also a patron of Cal Tech, funding two laboratories there.

KERN
Kern County, **Kernville**, the **Kern River** and **Kern Valley** are named for Edward Kern (1823-1863). Born in Philadelphia, he was the youngest of three brothers who were survey artists, and he participated in several key expeditions to the West. He served as topographer on Frémont's third expedition that crossed the Plains and Rockies to California in 1846. Near this spot at the confluence of the north and south forks of the Kern River, the expedition party camped for several weeks where Kern mapped the river and, as legend has it, Kern nearly drowned in the turbulent waters, prompting Frémont to name it after him. After his service with Fremont, he joined an expedition to Asia and the Pacific islands, before returning to Philadelphia to open a painting studio.

KETTLEMAN CITY
The San Joaquin Valley city stands on what was once the western edge of Tulare Lake. Its history begins with David H. Kettelman (1826-1916), a German immigrant who first came to Chicago in 1835 and then sailed around the horn for San Francisco in 1850. He tried his hand unsuccessfully at prospecting for gold before operating a general store. After deciding to raise cattle, he sold the store and moved south to what would be called the **Kettleman Hills,** where he grazed his stock which he sold to miners. In 1868 he finally settled in an area in what would become the town of Lodi where he built and developed a profitable cattle and

grain ranch and where he remained the rest of his life.

In the early 1900s the area was opened to developers, one of the latter, Manford Brown, bought a few hundred acres in 1929, subdividing a portion and naming it Kettleman City.

KEYES
The Stanislaus County town, part of greater Modesto, is thought to have been named in 1897 for Thomas J. Keyes (1823-1895), elected from the area to the California Assembly and Senate four times between 1854 and 1873.

KING CITY
The city is named for pioneer Charles Henry King (1842-1910) who, in 1884, purchased 13,000 acres of a land grant and founded the King Ranch. He introduced wheat to the Salinas Valley and was so successful that the Southern Pacific Railroad extended its lines to his ranch in 1886. Soon a flour mill was erected next to his warehouse and "King's Station" began to function as a commercial entity and, in time, a city. He was the youngest of, according to one account, fourteen brothers and sisters. At about ten, he went to Pittsburgh and worked as a "printer's devil," saving his money. Barely in his teens, he journeyed to California, had a brief, albeit unprofitable and exhausting, trial at mining for gold. He moved to San Francisco where he achieved financial success. In 1880, he moved to Oakland, where he became a developer and philanthropist.

Clarence King

KING, MOUNT CLARENCE

The flamboyant King (1842-1901)—whom Theodore Roosevelt's Secretary of State, John Hay, called "the best and brightest man of his generation"--is remembered by Californians today as the author of the classic *Mountaineering in the Sierra Nevada* (1871). After graduating from Yale, he attended glaciology lectures given by Louis Agassiz at Harvard. King then joined Josiah Whitney's California Geological Survey and made many first ascents in the Sierra and named such summits as Dana, Brewer, Lyell, and Whitney as sell as "King." In 1872 he uncovered one of the greatest financial frauds of the century: the Great Diamond Hoax, in which claims of a diamond field in Wyoming turned out to be a sham. In 1880 he became the first director of the U. S. Geological Survey. His remarkable personal life in set out in *Passing Strange: A Gilded Age Tale of Love and Deception Across the Color Line* (2009) by Martha A. Sandweiss.

At 13,000 feet, King's mountain is the high point of a divide north of Kings Canyon known as King Spur. It was originally dubbed Mount King in 1864 by the Whitney Survey, but later changed to Mount Clarence King.

KINGS BEACH

This stretch of North Lake Tahoe sprung into being in

131

1925 when Joe King allegedly acquired the town site after an all-night poker game with George Whittell, Jr., at the latter's grand estate at the Lake, the Thunderbird Lodge. Whittell was something of an eccentric with exotic tastes from the wild animals he kept as pets to the many mistresses he was said to maintain. At one time Whittell bought twenty-four acres of unspoiled wilderness along the Lake with the intention of developing casinos and housing projects. Some historians believe that it was not Whittell from whom King won the land, whose holdings were on the Nevada side, but wealthy San Francisco real estate developer Robert Sherman. In either event, King went on to grow the land from five small cabins to the thriving beach town of Kings Beach.

KNOTT'S BERRY FARM

The 160-acre theme park in the Orange County town of Buena Vista grew out of roadside stand selling berries grown by farmer Walter Knott (1889-1981) in the 1920s. In the next decade he and his wife opened a chicken dinner restaurant that became popular and eventually expanded into today's huge amusement park.

KRUSE RHODODENDRON STATE NATURAL RESERVE

The land for the 317-acre park in Sonoma County was donated by Edward P. Kruse in 1933 as a living memorial to his father, Edward T. Kruse (1829-1886), a founder of The German Savings and Loan Society of San Francisco and president of the Society of California Pioneers (open to direct descendants of a settler who was in California before 1850). Born in Germany, at the age of twenty, without much more capital than would carry him across the ocean, he sailed to San Francisco, arriving in 1849. As with almost every other young man embarking there he headed for the gold "diggings" where, at Paradise Bar, he opened a store. After a few years he sold it and moved to San Francisco, starting one of the first wholesale grocery businesses in the city.

Originally included in the *Rancho German*, the present

reserve later formed part of the large ranch established in 1880, on which the Kruse family raised sheep and carried on logging and tanbark harvesting operations.

KYBURZ

The Switzerland-born Samuel Kyburz (1810-1898) and his parents migrated to the United States in 1833, eventually settling in Wisconsin, where he married and took up farming. A few years later he and his family moved to Independence, Missouri, where they joined up with a wagon train going west, ending up at Sutter's Fort. Sutter hired Kyburz as overseer of his colony. In 1847 he picked a site in Coloma for Sutter and his partner, James Marshall, to build a sawmill. It was there the latter discovered gold on January 24, 1848. With the chaos of the ensuing Gold Rush, Kyburz left the fort for San Francisco where he had little luck as a merchant, eventually moving to Sacramento to run a hotel. In 1862 a calamitous flood drove his family from the city. They settled in El Dorado County, where he worked as manager of a roadhouse. After his death, one of his sons, Albert Burrows Kyburz (1852-1937), then living in Placerville, bought 120 acres in what is now Cameron Park. In 1900 he traded the property for a resort near Silver Fork. Also known as Sugarloaf, Slippery Ford, and other names, it became known as Kyburz in 1911 when the Post Office wanted to rename it when they were establishing its first office there. Albert, upon becoming the first postmaster, recommended that it be named in his father's memory.

L

LAFAYETTE

Benjamin Shreve came to what would become Lafayette, but was called at the time Acalanus, after his failure as a miner in the Gold Rush. In 1857 he became the town's postmaster and wanted to give it a new name. He requested the name of "Centerville" which was rejected because there was already a town of that name in California. He then asked for "La Fayette" after the French soldier and statesman. In 1932 the spelling was changed to "Lafayette"

In 1777 the Marquis de Lafayette (1757-1854) purchased a ship and, with a crew of adventurers, set sail for America to fight in the revolution against the British. He joined the ranks as a major general, assigned to the staff of George Washington. He served with distinction, leading American forces to several victories. On a return visit to France in 1779, Lafayette persuaded the French government to send aid to the Americans. After the British surrender at Yorktown, Lafayette returned to Paris, but remained a hero to the Americans.

LANARE

The name of the Fresno County town is taken from L(lewelyn) A(rthur) Nares (1860-1939). Born in England, he moved to Canada in 1879 where he became prominent in the development of Canadian interests. Moving to the United States a few years larer he invested in the irrigation canals on the north side of the Kern River. The colonization of these lands lead to further purchases and subsequent development. The town of Lanare was named after him by its settlers out of a respect for his contributions to the area. During the first world war he served as the food administrator in the San Joaquin Valley and in 1918 was appointed to survey the proposed transcontinental highway from Reno to Sal Lake City.

LANGLEY, MOUNT

The 14,042-foot peak was confused for several years with Mount Whitney. In 1871 Clarence King climbed the summit of what he thought to be the peak that he had named Mount Whitney. An account states that "we rode our mules to the highest crest of the peak southwest of Lone Pine, which for over three years now, has been known by the name of Mount Whitney, and which was ascended and measured as such by Mr. Clarence King, in the summer of 1871. . . . Certain it is, however, that the peak which for over three years has borne the name of Whitney, has done so only by mistake, and that a new name must be found for it; while the name of Whitney must now go back to the peak to which it was originally given in 1864, and which is, in reality, the highest and grandest of this culminating cluster of the Sierra Nevada." The peak was called Mount Corcoran by the artist Albert Bierstadt. As "Sheep Mountain," the name by which it was commonly known, was not sufficiently distinctive, the name Langley was placed on it in 1905.

Samuel Pierpont Langley (1834-1906) was a professor of astronomy and physics at Western University of Pennsylvania and secretary of the Smithsonian Institution (1887-1906). In 1881 he led an expedition to Mount Whitney for researches in solar heat.

135

LASSEN COUNTY/PEAK

Both the mountain and the county are named for Peter Lassen (1800-1859), a Danish émigré who arrived in 1830 at Boston where he worked as a blacksmith. He continued westward, first to Philadelphia, then to Missouri. where he remained until 1839, when he left with a small group for the west coast, finally making it to Sutter's Ranch, site of present-day Sacramento. He was appointed a member of a posse during an incident there: Two horses had been stolen and Lassen's group went to the northern Sacramento Valley to retrieve them. There he came upon the confluence of the Sacramento River and Deer Creek. Taken with that landscape, he obtained Mexican citizenship, allowing him to own property, and was soon granted 22,000 acres at Deer Creek. In February, 1845, his Bosquejo Ranch was established there, becoming the northernmost settlement in California. In 1847 Lassen went back to Missouri to recruit settlers for his new community. In the spring of 1848 he returned with a small group of emigrants, the first to cross over the Lassen Trail, by what would be named Lassen Peak or Mount Lassen.. After some financial reversals, he relocated to Indian Valley, Plumas County. In 1855 Lassen found gold in the Honey Lake Valley, where he settled in. In 1858, news circulated of the silver discovery in the Black Rock Desert, Nevada. In the spring of 1859, Lassen organized a prospecting party. One evening his camp was awakened by a gunshots, one killing Lassen. The identity of the murderer remains a mystery.

LATHROP

Located in the northern San Joaquin Valley in the Stockton metro area the city is generally credited to be named for Charles Lathrop (1849-1914), the brother-in-law of Leland Stanford, the former governor of California, railroad baron, and founder of Stanford University, though some sources claim that it was in honor of his wife Jane's maiden name. He later told her brother that it was named after him. A few years later he told an old college friend,

Lathrop Tracy, that he named Lathrop and Tracy after him. Another source states that it was named for another brother of his wife, Ariel Lathrop. The city father's have gone with Charles. He came to California from New York in 1877 working in San Francisco before joining Ariel in the management of Stanford's business affairs. When Stanford University was founded the scope of their activity was enlarged to include its affairs. After Stanford's death in 1893, his widow appointed her brother a trustee and made him treasurer and manager of the University, which positions he held until his death in 1914.

LATON
Present-day Laton in Fresno County was once part of the almost 50,000-acre Mexican land grant *Rancho Laguna de Tache*. It was purchased by San Feranciso business man, Charles A. Laton and L. A. Nares in 1896. The first post office opened in in 1900.

LATROBE
The name honors Benjamin Henry Latrobe, Jr. (1806-1878), the Chief Engineer of the Baltimore & Ohio Railroad who constructed many bridges, viaducts, and roadbeds in the eastern United States. The town was laid out in southwest El Dorado County in 1864 at the end of the Placerville-Sacramento Valley Railroad. In its first years it prospered as a way station for the commerce that streamed over the Placerville Road to Virginia City.

LAYTONVILLE
F. B. Layton started a blacksmith business in the one-time settlement of Cahto, in Mendocino County, but after a quarrel with town authorities in 1874 he up and moved about three miles northeast and built another shop and a home, from which Laytonville sprang.

LEANDRO, SAN
In 1842 José Joaquin Estudillo, a retired Spanish soldier, was granted 7,000 acres in Alameda County, which he named *Rancho San Leandro* after his patron saint. In 1855

137

his son-in-law filed a map of a town site to be called San Leandro, founded for the sole purpose of housing the Alameda County seat. Saint Leander (534-600), was a Benedictine monk who became Bishop of Seville and converted the Visigoths to Catholicism.

Joseph Le Conte

LeCONTE, MOUNT

Named in 1895 in honor of the first professor of geology at the University of California, the Sierra peak reaches a height of 13,390 feet. Joseph Le Conte (1823-1901) was born and educated in Georgia where he practiced medicine for a few years before deciding to go to Harvard and study natural history under Louis Agassiz. He then returned home where he taught geology for seventeen years, before joining the faculty at the University of California at Berkeley in 1869 where he remained until 1901. Aside from an eminent academic career, he was active in the preservation of the Sierra Nevada, co-founding the Sierra Club with John Muir and others in 1892 and serving on its board of directors for six years.

LEE VINING

Leroy Vining (1823-1863) and his brother were among the first prospectors that descended into the Mono Basin in 1852 after news of a gold strike and began digging in his namesake canyon. He did not find any gold, but he did make a fortune in timber after building a mill and selling lumber to local mining towns. His luck, unfortunately, came to an abrupt end in Aurora. After making a delivery, he died from a gunshot wound to the groin. Although the details are not clear, it seems that the small Derringer gun that he carried in his front pocket accidentally discharged and Vining bled to death. The town was not laid out until 1926 and was named "Lakeview." When it was later learned that another California town was using the name, Lee Vining was selected.

LEIMERT PARK
This Los Angeles neighborhood is named for Walter H. Leimert (1877-1970). The son of German immigrants, he came to Los Angeles in the early 1920s and began to develop planned communities. He began construction of Leimert Park in 1928 as one of the first comprehensively planned communities in the Southland.

LEMOORE
Dr. Lavern Lee Moore (1822-1898) first made his home north of Tulare Lake in what is now Kings County in 1871. He decided to knit together the scores of surrounding farm families in order to secure a post office He also hoped to attract the railroad, which was then being planned but was not built until six years later. The following year he established the first real estate development in this district and had laid out and named the streets after other pioneer families. Land auctions were held and lots went to the highest bidder. Within the year a signed petition was sent to the U.S. Post Office Department for a post office in the new town to be called Lemoore, a fanciful contraction of the founder's names. The nearby 30,000-acre **Naval Air Station Leemoore** is the Navy's largest, and only west coast, Master Jet base.

LEONA VALLEY
The original name of the small unincorporated rural town near Palmdale was Leonis Valley, named after Miguel Leonis (1824-1889), a colorful Basque sheep and cattle

139

rancher who claimed land from Leonis Valley to Calabasas and was often referred to as "El Basque Grandee" and the "King of Calabasas." He arrived in the area in 1858 with hardly a penny to his name and by the time of his death he was the third richest man in California and owner of over ten-thousand acres of land. Leonis was often in trouble with the law, hiring gunmen to expand his lands, bribing witnesses and threatening nearby settlers. He was killed in 1889 when he fell from his wagon after removing a band of squatters from his property.

LIMANTOUR BEACH

The long, narrow strand between Drakes Bay and an estuary at Point Reyes National Seashore is named for a French merchant based in Mexico who traded at various Pacific ports, Joseph Yves Limantour (1812-1885). The beach took his name when one of his schooners ran aground there in 1851 causing Limantour to be stuck in California for a few years. In 1853 he made the astounding claim before the Federal Land Commission that the Mexican government had granted him about 200,000 acres of land, including much of the city of San Francisco! The claim proved to be based on fraud and Limantour was arrested, but, after raising bail, fled to Mexico.

LINCOLN

The western Placer County city sprung from a vision by the young civil engineer Theodore D. Judah of a new town. He surveyed the area for the Sacramento Valley Railroad and held title to the site of the planned railhead. But when funding problems temporarily halted track construction, Judah sold his property to the railroad's president, Charles Lincoln Wilson (1803-1890). Within weeks the San Francisco executive had mapped out a town site which he named Lincoln after his own middle name. In 1859 Wilson sold 46 lots at auction. Wilson had come to California in 1849 and built the first plank road in San Francisco in 1850. He was the promoter and builder of the first railroad in California and became president of the Sacramento Valley Railroad.

LINCOLN HEIGHTS

Originally called East Los Angeles, it later took its present name when Lincoln High School was built in 1878 and named for President Abraham Lincoln (1809-1865), assassinated thirteen years earlier.

LINDSAY

Capt. Arthur J. Hutchinson, the founder of the Tulare County city, came to the San Joaquin Valley in 1889. He was born in Bermuda, where his father was assigned by the British government and served for a time as governor. Capt. Hutchinson was a Royal Military College graduate and served in India until 1879, when illness forced his retirement. Coming to California for his health, he moved to the Lindsay area, bought 2,000 acres and formed the Lindsay Land Company. When the Southern Pacific Railroad came through the area in 1889, development of the Lindsay town site began under the Pacific Development Company. It was laid out by Capt. Hutchinson and the community was named for his wife, Sadie Lindsay Patton Hutchinson (1863-19??). She had met her husband when he was visiting her father at the family's Virginia plantation and were married in 1888.

LITTLE STATE NATURAL RESERVE, JOHN

Probably the least-known park at Big Sur contains a short section of cliffs and bluffs around the lower end of Lime Creek, west of Highway 1 and just south of the Esalen Institute buildings at Slate's Hot Springs. It contains the original 1917 cabin of early conservationist Elizabeth King Livermore, who donated the land to the state in 1952. She specified that it be named for John Little (18??-1928), a cattle rancher who was born in Monterey, the son of Milton Little, Sr. who in 1850 owned all of New Monterey, 300 acres of hillside overlooking Cannery Row and Monterey Bay. John moved to Big Sur and, through homesteading and "buying out" other settlers, came to own hundreds of acres, including Slate's Hot Springs, which he homesteaded and to which he received title in

1902. Livermore, often described as "a Marin County socialite," acquired land in the area by researching title to unclaimed land, then filing on them herself. She thus became owner of a parcel adjoining Slate's Hot Springs where she had built a vacation home. She and Little were "close friends" according to neighbors.

LIVERMORE

Robert Livermore (1799-1858), an English sailor, jumped ship in 1822 in California and "went native," marrying a Spanish woman and becoming a naturalized citizen of Alta California. In 1839 the governor granted him land in Alameda County in what was later called **Livermore Valley** where he began to raise cattle and to which he added additional property, until he owned about 40,000 acres, making him a wealthy man. After the discovery of gold in California, the area became a popular stopping place for prospectors headed for the Mother Lode. Livermore died before the establishment of the town that bears his name. His ranch included much of the present-day city, which was established in 1869 by William Mendenhall (1823-1911) who had met Livermore while marching through the valley with Frémont's California Battalion in 1846.

LIVINGSTON

According to the official City of Livingston website, the Merced County town was originally to be named after the famed African explorer Dr. Livingstone whose disappearance at the time created world-wide publicity. The town was laid out by platting a visionary 80 blocks, 40 blocks on each side of the railroad track, with the hope that the large number of blocks would make Livingston the county seat. Lots of 25 by 125 feet were offered for $1.00 if Livingstone were chosen. In 1872 the town lost the election for a new county seat to Merced by 200 votes. In 1873, in a petition for a new post office, the final letter "E" was inadvertently deleted and the town officially became Livingston.

LOCKEFORD

Dean J. Locke (1823-1887), a New Hampshire native and Harvard Medical school-trained physician, came to San Joaquin County in 1849. With his two brothers he bought 360 acres of land along the Mokelumne River for a dollar an acre and built a ranch. The town was later laid out on the ranch property and christened Lockeford by Dr. Locke's wife, who suggested the name as people called the river-crossing "Locke's ford."

LOGAN HEIGHTS

The San Diego neighborhood and the adjacent community of **Barrio Logan** take their names from a street in the area named in 1881 for John A. Logan (1826-1886). After serving as a General in Union Army during the Civil War, he went into Illinois politics and served as a State Senator, Congressman and U. S. Senator. He was also an unsuccessful candidate for the Vice-Presidency. In 1871 he authored legislation to provide subsidies for a transcontinental railroad to end at San Diego, presumably the act that got a street named for him in that city.

LOOMIS

The Placer County city was named after one of its pioneers, James Loomis (1830-1895), who worked as railroad agent, saloon keeper, and postmaster. Loomis came to California in 1852 from his native Detroit. It was incorporated in 1984 to prevent annexation by neighboring Rocklin. It was originally named Pino, but had to be changed in 1890 in order to avoid confusion with Reno.

LONDON STATE HISTORIC PARK, JACK

The park is a memorial to the Oakland-born writer and adventurer Jack London (1876-1916) who lived in a cottage at the Sonoma County site—once part of his Beauty Ranch--from 1905 until his death. His wife, Charmian, continued to live in the cottage there until her death in 1955.

LORENZO, SAN

The name of the Alameda County city stems from *El Arroyo San Lorenzo*, now known as San Lorenzo Creek, the name being first recorded in 1770 in the journal of Lt. Pedro Fages of the Portolá expedition. Mexico granted the land to Guillermo Castro who, during the Gold Rush era, sold the land to the many squatters who had settled along the creek. The federal government accepted the name San Lorenzo with the opening of the community's post office. San Lorenzo (225-258)--Spanish for "Saint Lawrence"—is one of the most honored martyrs of the Roman Catholic church, put to death in Rome by the emperor Valerian.

LOS ANGELES

The nation's Second City is not the "City of Angels," rather it is named for a particular person: Mary, the mother of Jesus. However, what the exact original name was of the city has become somewhat muddled in history. In 1769, diarist Father Juan Crespí named the Los Angeles River and surrounding valley *El Río Valle de la Nuestra Señora de los Angeles de Porciuncula*, on the feast day of Our Lady of the Angels of the Porciuncula Chapel in Italy, where St. Francis of Assisi founded the Franciscan order. Twelve years later, when a town was founded on the banks of the river, it was named *El Pueblo de la Reyna de Los Angeles*, meaning "the town of the Queen of the Angels." Some historians believe that the city's correct original name is *El Pueblo de Nuestra Senora de los Angeles de Porciuncula*, or "the town of Our Lady of the Angels of Porciuncula." Whether it is the "Queen" or "Our Lady," it is clear that it refers to Mary, who is known by both of those titles. It has also become academic, as the city is now known simply as "Los Angeles."

On the northern rim of the city is **Angeles National Forest**, designated in 1892 as the first national forest in the state. It was initially called San Gabriel Timberland Reserve, but was renamed in 1907.

LUCIA MOUNTAINS, SANTA

Vizcaíno gave the name *Sierra de la Santa Lucia*, to the range extending over Monterey and San Luis Obispo Counties, in honor of the saint whose day (December 13th) had just been celebrated. According to her hagiography, Saint Lucy (282-304) was a Christian during the Diocletian persecution. She consecrated her virginity to God, refused to marry a pagan, and had her dowry given to the poor. Her would-be husband denounced her as a Christian to the governor of Syracuse, Sicily. Miraculously unable to move her or burn her, the guards took out her eyes with a fork. She is the patron saint of the blind.

LUIS OBISPO, SAN

The City and County of San Luis Obispo began with the founding of *Misíon San Luís Obispo de Tolosa* in 1772 by Father Junípero Serra as the fifth California mission. It is named after Saint Louis, (1274-1297) son of the King of Naples, who became a Franciscan friar. At the age of twenty-two he was consecrated Bishop of Toulouse, France. His tenure was brief, for on his return journey the following year from a visit to his sister, the Queen of Aragon, he took ill and died. He was considered a patron of the monastery in Majorca, the home of Serra and Crespí. The city and county take their names from the mission.

LUKENS, MOUNT

Located on the eastern boundary of Los Angeles, it is the highest peak within the city limits. Its namesake, Theodore Parker Lukens (1848-1918), was a Pasadena civic and business leader and an early supporter of the reforestation effort in California. He was Pasadena's first real estate developer and a two-term mayor (1890-92 and 1894-96). A self-taught botanist, Lukens believed that burnt-over mountainsides could be successfully replanted. During 1899 alone, Lukens and fellow mountaineers planted some 65,000 seeds in the mountains above Pasadena. After his death, the 5,074-foot peak was named to honor the one-time Angeles National Forest Supervisor and Southern California's "Father of Forestry."

LYELL, MOUNT

The highest peak in Yosemite National Park was named in 1863 by the California Geological Survey for British geologist Sir Charles Lyell (1797-1875). In his famous *Principles of Geology* (1830-33), he conclusively demonstrated that the earth was much older than believed and had changed its form slowly, mainly from conditions such as erosion. Lyell was able to date the ages of rocks by using fossils embedded in the stone as indicators of time. Darwin later used Lyell's data in constructing his theory of evolution. Brewer wrote in his classic journal, *Up and Down California in 1860-1864* (1930): "As we had named the other mountain Mount Dana, after the most eminent of American geologists, we named this Mount Lyell, after the most eminent of English geologists."

LYNWOOD

The Los Angeles County city traces its name to 1902 when pioneer dairyman Charles H. Sessions bought about four hundred acres and started a business which he named "The Lynwood Dairy and Creamery" in honor of his wife, Lynne Wood Sessions. A few years later Southern Pacific established a siding there, which it called the "Lynwood Siding." In 1913 a group of investors formed the Lynwood Company to develop home sites which they sold for $500 to $800. It was incorporated in 1921.

M

McCLOUD RIVER

In 1829 a group of Canadian Hudson Bay Company trappers and explorers, led by Alexander Roderick McLeod (1782-1840), were the first European-Americans to travel through the northern California valley through which the river runs. The expedition had nearly disastrous results. While returning to Oregon after nearly a year trapping in California, the party was caught in a series of winter storms near the headwaters of the McCloud River, After being trapped for over a month, the party had to abandon its cache of over 2400 beaver and otter pelts, their horses, and make a desperate attempt to save their lives.

The timber town of **McCloud** took root in 1897 with the founding of the McCloud River Railroad Company which made it economically feasible to transport lumber to population centers.

McCLURES BEACH

The Point Reyes beach is named for James McClure (1869-1934) who emigrated from Ireland in 1889 and began a dairy farm on property which included the beach, and has continued to the present day, on 1400-acres in the Point Reyes National Seashore Park. The National Park Service bought the McClure Dairy in 1971 and offered the family a long-term lease to continue farming the land. The family gifted some of their coastal property—known today as McClure's Beach—to the Service.

McCONNELL STATE RECREATION AREA
Livingston real estate and insurance broker Warren F. McConnell (1894-1966) and his wife, Lillian, donated Merced County land to the State in 1949; it had formerly been part of the family ranch started by his grandfather in 1852. With its opening in 1950 the 74-acre recreation area along the Merced River became the first state park in the San Joaquin Valley.

McFARLAND
James Boyd McFarland came to California from Zanesville, Ohio, where he taught school, and settled in Anaheim. While visiting northern Kern County in 1907, he took a liking to the area known as Hunt's Siding. He bought fifty acres, subdivided it, and built houses. He was instrumental in bringing water to the town named for him, which sparked its growth. He later served on the County Board of Supervisors.

McGRATH STATE BEACH
Situated between Ventura and Oxnard, it is named for Dominick McGrath (1827-1908) who came from Ireland to California in 1848 and found his fortune not in gold but by selling hides, mutton and wool in the gold fields. He bought over a thousand acres of land near the mouth of the Santa Clara River and started a farm. His descendants sold 295 acres of it to the State in 1961 which became a State Beach the following year.

MacKERRICHER STATE PARK
A few miles north of Fort Bragg on the Mendocino coast, it was sold to the State in 1949 by the heirs of Duncan

McKerricher (1836-1926), a Canadian homesteader who had settled in the area in 1865. A few years later he was able to purchase a thousand acres which he called *Rancho de la Laguna* and where he carried on dairy and livestock operations.

McKINLEYVILLE
One of the original communities that constitute the present Humboldt County town was called Minor or Minorville. In 1901 President William McKinley (1843-1901) was assassinated. To honor him the town changed its name to McKinleyville.

MAILLIARD REDWOODS STATE NATURAL RESERVE
It is named for conservationist John Ward Mailliard Jr. (1891-1954), a third-generation San Franciscan who had been an active member of the Save-the-Redwood League. He began buying ranch land in the Mendocino area after honeymooning there in 1916; it became the center of much of his family's life and surrounded the present Reserve. He sat on over twenty company boards and city commissions while overseeing the family business, Mailliard & Schmeidell. As a member of the Republican Central Committee, he was a key advisor to Governor Earl Warren in the nineteen-forties.

MANLY PEAK
Quietly isolated, Manly Peak stands at 7,196 feet on the boundary between Death Valley National Park and **Manly Peak Wilderness** (designated by Congress in 1994). It is named for William Lewis Manly (1820-1903), author of the Gold Rush classic *Death Valley in '49* (1894), an account of the trek he and John Rogers made from the floor of Death Valley across mountain and desert wastes to the Pacific coast and their return. Manly finally settled in the Santa Clara Valley.

MARCH FIELD
The air base ten miles southwest of Riverside began at a

149

time when the United States was rushing to build up its military forces in anticipation of its entry into World War I. On March 20, 1918, Alessandro Flying Training Field became March Field, named in honor of Second Lieutenant Peyton C. March, Jr. (1896-1918), son of the Army Chief of Staff, who had been killed in a flying accident in Texas the previous month, just two weeks after being commissioned. He is buried at Arlington National Cemetery. In 1996 it became officially known as March Air Reserve Base.

MARCOS, SAN
The San Diego County city takes its name from *Los Vallecitos de San Marcos* ("Little Valleys of Saint Mark") named by the Portolá Expedition in 1797 to honor the day of discovery, the feast day of Saint Mark, the first century author of the second Gospel.

MARGARITA, RANCHO SANTA
Spanish explorer Gasper de Portolá first scouted the area in 1769, naming the Santa Margarita Valley in Orange County in honor of the virgin martyr St. Margaret of Antioch. Her exact dates are not known but she is thought to have lived during the persecutions by the Roman Emperor Diocletian in the third century. Her father was a pagan priest who disowned her when he learned of her conversion to Christianity. She became a shepherdess to support herself but got caught up in the imperial net of persecution when she refused to wed a young officer since she had made a vow of chastity.

The Franciscan fathers founded Mission San Juan Capistrano in 1776, and ruled the region until 1821, when California became part of Mexico. The Mexican governors carved the area around the mission into three large ranchos: *Rancho Trabuco, Rancho Mission Viejo*, and *Rancho Santa Margarita*. The area remained fairly remote until 1986, when the first homes in the new master planned community of Rancho Santa Margarita were sold. In 1999 area voters opted to incorporate the Rancho Santa Margarita Planned Community and the neighboring

Robinson Ranch, Dove Canyon, Rancho Cielo, Trabuco Highlands and Walden Communities as the City of Rancho Santa Margarita.

MARGARITA, SANTA
The remote town grew out of the *Santa Margarita de Cortona Asistencia* founded as an outpost of the San Luis Obispo Mission in 1797. Its namesake, Santa Margarita (1247-1297), was a "fallen woman" who came to conversion in Cortona, Italy and lived the rest of her life in poverty as a Franciscan penitent. She was canonized in 1728.

Nearby **Santa Margarita Lake** was created with the construction of the Salinas Dam in 1941 and is now a major source of drinking water for the city of San Luis Obispo.

MARIA, SANTA
Juan Pacífico Ontiveros and his wife, María, arrived in north Santa Barbara County in 1855 and built a palatial adobe at the mouth of a local canyon and called their home Santa María in honor of the Virgin Mary. He had already named the nearby waterway "Santa Maria Creek," until it rained for a month straight in 1861 and then he referred to it as a river. Today is called the **Santa Maria River** and the surrounding region the **Santa Maria Valley**. The city was first called Grangerville, then Central City, but in 1885 at the behest of the postal authorities—to avoid confusion with a city of the same name in Colorado--the town fathers came up with "Santa Maria" from the name that Ontiveros had given to his property thirty years earlier.

MARIN COUNTY
The name is derived from the Coast Miwok Chief Marin (1781-1835) of the Licatiut Tribe who lived in the area. In 1815 a Spanish military expedition explored the land north of San Francisco Bay, an action which angered the tribe, and a battle was fought in what is now known as the Petaluma Valley. Chief Marin's leadership and bravery were admired by the Spanish. He was later converted to

Christianity and baptized under the name of "El Marinero" or "Marino" because of his knowledge of the Bay, on which he often acted as ferryman for the Spaniards. The name was "corrupted" over time to "Marin." He later became an *alcalde* at Mission San Rafael after its establishment in 1817. In 1821 he was a guide for a Spanish expedition to the north, but soon afterwards, as California transitioned from Spain to Mexico, he was written up as "insubordinate." The *Californio* Mariano Vallejo named Marin County for the chief in 1850.

MARINO, SAN

The San Gabriel Valley community takes its name from the *rancho* named by its owner after his grandfather's plantation in Maryland which had received its name from the Republic of San Marino in Europe. Tradition holds that the latter was named for a fourth-century saint, Marinus, a stonemason who worked at Monte Titano in modern San Marino. He was a lay preacher who ministered to Christians who had been sentenced to quarry work as punishment for their faith. Though he belonged to no order that required it, he was a life-long bachelor. Falsely accused by an insane woman of Rimini of being her estranged husband, he fled to a cave on Monte Titano and lived there as a hermit.

MARKLEEVILLE

Separated from the rest of California by the escarpment of the Sierra Nevada, the seat of Trinity County—California's smallest—traces its beginnings to the land claim of Jacob J. Marklee or Markley (1830-1863), a Canadian-born settler who left his wife and family in Minnesota in 1861 for California, building a cabin in what is today Markleeville, where he built a toll bridge across a tributary of the Carson River during the height of the silver mining boom at nearby Silver Mountain City, Nevada. He hoped to enrich himself from the freight and supplies bound for the mining camps, but was instead murdered in 1863, the killer being acquitted on the grounds of self defense.

MARKS STATE PARK, THE FOREST OF NISENE
In 1890 Nisene Marks (18??-1955) and her husband, Benjamin, purchased a 2000-acre property in the Salinas Valley. Shortly after they settled, Benjamin died, leaving Nisene to raise their four children. She was able to create one of the largest egg ranches in California during the first half of the 20th century, all on her own. Between 1951 and 1954 the Marks family purchased the holdings of the Loma Prieta Lumber Company near Aptos in Santa Cruz County as well as a number of adjacent parcels until they owned approximately 9000 acres. Following the death of Nisene in 1955, her children decided to establish a state park as a living memorial. The result was the Forest of Nisene Marks State Park, founded in 1963. More than 1000 acres have been added to the park through the efforts of the Save-the-Redwoods League

MARTINEZ
In 1824 Ygnacio Martinez (1774-1848), the early nineteenth century *commandante* of the Presidio of San Francisco (1822-1827), received a 17,000-acre land grant from the Mexican government—*Rancho El Pinole* on the southern bank of Carquinez Strait. It was from this grant that the City of Martinez later rose. It was named for Don Ygnacio in 1849.

MARYSVILLE
Charles Covillaud, a Frenchman, owned an interest in a ranch on the land that would later become Marysville, on the confluence of the Feather and Yuba Rivers. During the Gold Rush it became a point of debarkation for riverboats from San Francisco and Sacramento filled with miners on their way to the dig sites. It grew and Covillaud and the men to whom he had later sold part of his ranch decided to create a master plan for a town. It was decided to name it after Covillaud's new wife, Mary Murphy (1831-1867). who as a teenager had survived the Donner Party disaster of 1847 and settled at Sutter's Fort. As a result of the Gold Rush, Marysville grew, until by 1854 it was the third largest city in California with nearly 10,000 people.

MAXWELL

The town in the center of Colusa County started off as Occident, but with the opening of the first post office in 1855 with local landowner and saloonkeeper George Maxwell (1828-1879) as postmaster and, presumably, the donor of the local site for the Northern Railway Depot, its name was changed to Maxwell.

MAYWOOD

The Laguna Land & Water Company began subdividing the Los Angeles County property which would constitute the community in 1919 and sent out cards to the purchasers asking them to vote on a name for the town. It seemed that one of the developers' employees, May Wood, was so popular that her name was selected by the voters and became official in 1924 when the town was incorporated.

MEINERS OAKS

The community is named for John Meiners (1827-1898) who came to America from Germany in 1848, not to California in search of gold, but to Milwaukee in search of liquid gold—beer brewing. Home of many German breweries, he found success there and became a wealthy man. He acquired a ranch in the Ojai Valley of Ventura County in the 1870s as a result of an unpaid debt. He came out to see his property and discovered he owned what was perhaps the largest oak grove on level land in Southern California. He built a ranch north of the grove and lived there off and on until his death, growing fruit and raising grain. It was later developed to offer affordable housing to homecoming soldiers at the end of World War II.

MENDOCINO

Both city and county derive their name from Cape Mendocino, which was discovered and named by Cabrillo in 1542 in honor of Don Antonio de Mendoza (1495-1552), Count of Tendilla, the first viceroy of New Spain, or Mexico, appointed by the King of Spain in 1535. It was Mendoza who had dispatched Cabrillo's expedition to

California. In 1550, after fifteen years of what was considered a model administration, Mendoza was sent to take up the post of viceroy in Peru. But he had little time to continue his work, dying within two years.

MENIFEE
Menifee Valley in Riverside County takes its name from Luther Menifee Wilson (1845-1899), a miner from Kentucky who in about 1880 discovered a large gold quartz lode there. He built a home and mined for several years before taking his profits and moving on. The planned communities of Sun City, Menifee Lakes, Quail Valley and Romoland all developed there and in 2008 incorporated as the City of Menifee.

MERCED
Named after the **Merced River**, which was initially named in 1806 by Gabriel Moraga *Rio de Nuestra Senora de la Merced*, meaning "the river of Our Lady of Mercy," that being another name for the Virgin Mary. The county, formerly part of Mariposa County, was named in 1855 while the city came into being when the Southern Pacific reached the site in 1872.

MERLO STATE RECREATION AREA, HARRY A.
Louisiana-Pacific Company, a major building products company, donated the land adjacent to the Humboldt Lagoons State Park to the State in the mid-1970s. It is named for the company's CEO at the time, Harry A. Merlo (b. 1925), who served in that capacity from 1972, the year it spun off from Georgia-Pacific, to 1995. He is also the founder of the World Forest Institute.

MERRITT, LAKE
In 1850 Dr. Samuel Merritt (1822-1890), a San Francisco physician originally from Maine, visited the East Bay. He was struck by the *Estero de San Antonio*—or, perhaps, his vision of what it could be. This encounter sowed the seeds to the creation of Lake Merritt. In 1854 Merritt purchased land along the shoreline of "the lake" and began to

155

cultivate the area. In 1863, he moved to Oakland and built a wharf and went into business selling building materials. Merritt prospered and, in 1867, became Oakland's mayor. In 1869 he completed a dam and bridge across the slough, replacing an earlier toll bridge. Merritt had for about 15 years been buying up the marshy land around the slough, so he did very well on his real estate investment. Although officially named Lake Peralta, it soon became popularly known as Merritt's Lake, later Lake Merritt, and the name eventually became the official one.

MEYER MEMORIAL STATE BEACH, ROBERT H.

Three west Malibu "pocket beaches" were bought by the State in 1976 and opened to the public in 1984. and named for State Park official Robert H. Meyer "in recognition of his contribution to the state park system."

MILLBRAE

A native New Yorker, Darius Ogden Mills (1825-1910) came to California in 1848 and opened a general store in Sacramento. Making enormous profits, he soon started up the bank of D.O. Mills and Company. In 1864, he went to San Francisco where he co-founded the Bank of California with William Ralston and was appointed its first president. Under his leadership, the bank invested in the silver mines of Nevada's Comstock Lode and as a result became one of the west's prominent financial institutions. In 1873 he resigned as president and Ralston was appointed in his place. Two years later, the Bank of California collapsed due to overspending, followed by Ralston's sudden death. Mills resumed the bank's presidency and within three years re-built it to its former strength. In 1878 he again resigned and moved back to New York. In the 1860s he had purchased land south of San Francisco in San Mateo County to build his country estate—Millbrae—from his surname and the Scottish word for "rolling hills." which he held on to and to where he retired. The community that developed around the estate took the name and was incorporated in 1948.

Joaquin Miller

MILLER PARK, JOAQUIN

The park grew out of the dream of Joaquin Miller (1837-1913), known as "The Byron of the Rockies" and "The Poet of the Sierra" for his extensive literary works, who came to California from Oregon around 1850. Dabbling in occupations from Indian fighter to pony-express rider to author to horse thief, he also was a tree lover and planter. In 1886 he purchased seventy barren acres in the hills above Oakland where he planted thousands of trees. The Oakland Parks Department bought this land from Miller, with the provision that his wife and daughter could live out their lives in homes he'd built for them there. Later, in 1928, nearby land was being eyed by developers, but action by the Save-the-Redwoods League helped to protect these trees, and the land was later purchased by the City of Oakland. This acreage, together with Miller's original property and nearby Sequoia Park, constitute Joaquin Miller Park today.

MILLER STATE SEASHORE, CLEM

The land stretching from the mouth of the Eel River to Pudding Creek at Fort Bragg honors Clement W. "Clem" Miller (1917-1962). Born in Delaware, he and his wife came to Marin County in 1948 and eventually made Corte Madera their home. He was elected to Congress (1958-

1962) for the State's First District comprised of Del Norte, Humboldt, Lake, Marin, Mendocino, Napa and Sonoma counties and was instrumental in passing the 1962 legislation designating Point Reyes a national seashore. Unfortunately, only weeks after President Kennedy signed it, he was killed in a plane crash in Del Norte County. The Clem Miller State Seashore was dedicated in 1994.

MILLERTON LAKE

The story begins with Fort Miller, situated on the south side of the San Joaquin River in the foothills of the Sierra Nevada in what was then part of Fresno County. It was named for Major Albert S. Miller (18??-1852), of the 2nd Infantry, a graduate of West Point, and veteran of the Black Hawk, Seminole, and Mexican Wars, who served at Monterey in 1849 and, in 1850, commanded an expedition to the Sierra. He died at the barracks in Benecia, which was under his command, a victim of alcoholism. Nearby a tent city called Millerton, named after the fort, sprouted and served as the county's first seat (1856-74), after which it was abandoned. The fort's site is now covered by Millerton Lake which was formed when the Friant Dam was built across the river canyon in 1944. It is now the **Millerton Lake State Recreation Area**.

MODJESKA CANYON

Helen Modjeska (1840-1909) was born in Krakow, Poland. By the time she was thirty, she became the leading actress of the Warsaw stage and had married a Polish aristocrat, Count Bozenta. The two of them dreamed of moving to America, he to start an agricultural colony, she to perform. they came in 1876 to Orange County. The émigres who joined them, though cultured—one was Henryk Sienkiewics, author of *Quo Vadis* (1895) and winner of the 1905 Nobel Prize for literature—were not practical farmers. Modjeska later recalled in her autobiography: "The most alarming feature of this bucolic fancy was the rapid disappearance of cash and the absence of even a shadow of income." Though the colony did not prosper, Modjeska's career did and she became a star of the stage.

In the 1880s, with the earnings from her career she purchased land in Santiago Canyon, which she called "Arden" after the forest in Shakespeare's *As You Like It*. She hired the famous architect Stanford White to design a home for her and her husband and where they would live for eighteen years. The area of Santiago Canyon where she lived is now called Modjeska Canyon.

MOFFETT FEDERAL AIRFIELD
Located in Santa Clara County at the southern tip of San Francisco Bay, the field, currently operated by NASA, encompasses 2,200 acres. Originally commissioned in 1933 as a base for the Navy's dirigibles, it was named for Rear Admiral William S. Moffett (1869-1933) the man usually credited with the field's development, who was killed the same year in a dirigible crash that took seventy-three lives during a storm off the New Jersey Coast. A Naval Academy graduate and a Medal of Honor winner, he headed the Navy's Aviation Bureau during the 1920s.

MOLERA STATE PARK, ANDREW
The land in the heart of Big Sur was part of the large *Rancho del Sur* that belonged to the Molera family. Andrew Molera (1897-1931) managed the ranch from 1915 until his death. He is credited for being among the first in California to commercially cultivate artichokes. This he did in the early 1920s on his land in Castroville. His sister Frances wanted to preserve the Big Sur land and arranged with the Nature Conservancy for it to hold the property until her death, with the intention that it then be turned into a state park named in memory of her brother. She died in 1968, and Andrew Molera State Park opened in 1972.

MONICA, SANTA
Legend has it that in 1769 the Franciscan Fr. Juan Crespí, part of Portolá's expedition party, inspired by a free-flowing natural spring named the area after Saint Monica (332-187), who wept for her wayward son, Saint Augustine, before he was converted from paganism to

Christianity. The seaside city adjacent to Los Angeles founded in 1875 is on the land that once part of Mexican land grant of *Rancho San Vicente y Santa Monica*. She is also the namesake of the **Santa Monica Mountains National Recreation Area.**

MONROVIA

William Newton Monroe (1841-1935) first brought his family to California in 1875 after a successful ten-year period of building railroads in the Midwest. A former school teacher and army officer during the Civil War, he met Charles Crocker of "Big Four" fame, who persuaded Monroe to relocate. The family set up headquarters in Los Angeles while Monroe was building railroads throughout the state for Southern Pacific. From 1879 to 1882 he served on the Los Angeles City Council. The Monroes began their search in Southern California for the perfect home site. They came to the San Gabriel Valley, where E.J. "Lucky" Baldwin had subdivided the eastern portion of his vast *Rancho Santa Anita* into thirty-acre parcels. In 1886 Monroe and a group of friends and associates bought ssome acreage on which they would establish a town which they would call "Monrovia: in honor of W. N. Monroe. on their combined holdings. In honor of W.N. Monroe,

MONTAGUE

Samuel Skerry Montague (1830-1883) is this Shasta Valley city's namesake. He is best remembered as the Chief Engineer of the Central Pacific Railroad Company at the time of the completion of the transcontinental railroad. The New Hampshire-born engineer had no academic training in the field; all his knowledge was learned on the job, starting with with the Rock Island and Rockford Railroad when he was twenty-two. Unsuccessful in his quest for gold in 1859 at Pike Peak, Colorado, he moved to California where he found work on the California Central Railroad, which was to run from Folsom to Marysville, through it never got beyond Lincoln. At the unexpected death of Central Pacific's chief engineer,

160

Theodore Judah, the twenty-six-year-old Montague took over the reins and was responsible for construction of the western half of the transcontinental line eastward to Omaha. He is one of the dignitaries pictured in "Last Spike," the famous painting of the 1869 completion ceremony. He was Chief Engineer for twenty years. He never lived in Montague, choosing to reside in Oakland.

MONTEREY
Sebastian Vizcaíno, leading a fleet consisting of the ships *San Diego* and *Santo Tomás*, and the frigate *Tres Reyes*, sailed past Carmel Bay and on December 16, 1602 rounded *Punta de los Pinos* and entered the harbor. They named the harbor after the viceroy of Mexico, Don Gaspár de Zúñiga y Acevedo, Count of Monte Rey, who had dispatched the expedition. They were the first known European explorers to reach Monterey. **Monterey Park** is a city in the environs of Los Angeles.

MONTGOMERY CREEK
The Shasta County town was named for Zachariah "Zach" Montgomery (1825-1900), a popular orator, politician and lawyer who supported the South in the Civil War and refused to take the California test oath on constitutional grounds. Born, raised, and trained in the law in Kentucky, he crossed the plains to California in 1850.. Not meeting with mining success, he returned to practicing law. He held several offices including member of the State Assembly and U.S. Attorney, He was the author of *Poison Drops in the Federal Senate: The School Question from a Parental and Non-Sectarian Standpoint* (1886) a jeremiad against compulsory school attendance laws.

MONTGOMERY WOODS STATE NATURAL RESERVE
The remote Mendocino County park began with a nine-acre donation by Robert Orr in 1945, and has been enlarged to almost 2,750 acres by donations and purchases by the Save-the-Redwoods association. The woods constituting the park were named for Andrew

161

Montgomery (1818-1910) who homesteaded the redwood grove when he came to Ukiah area in 1857 from Missouri over the Overland Trail. He served as Justice of the Peace for Ukiah Township from 1865 to 1867.

MORAGA VALLEY

The name memorializes Joaquin Moraga (1793- 1855), the grandson of Joseph Joaquin Moraga (1741-1785), who was second in command of the Anza expedition of 1776, and the founder and first *commandante* of the San Francisco Presidio. Joaquin, who served in the military with his father, Gabriel Moraga, at the Presidio, left the Army in 1819. He and his cousin, Juan Bernal, received a 13,316-acre land grant from the Mexican government in 1835. Known as *Rancho Laguna De Los Palos Colorados* (Ranch Of The Lake Of The Redwoods), the grant included parts of the present communities of Orinda and Lafayette as well as Canyon, Redwood, Rheem, and Moraga.

In 1841 Joaquin Moraga built an adobe on a hill overlooking what was being called Moraga Valley. In 1850 California became part of the United States and the Moraga family's claim had to be approved by the government. The land was granted to them in 1855 but the survey of the lands wasn't finished until 1876, so the Moragas had to keep fighting for their title over the land. Many feuds erupted in the 1870's as the Moragas tried to protect their land. By 1866 the Moragas had lost all of their land, but some descendants still lived inside the boundaries. Parts of the property were sold to pay taxes and a large share of the land was given to Moraga's former attorney in order to pay for services. Small portions were divided into ranches later made into residential areas.. In 1912 the bulk of the rancho was purchased by James Irvine. He started the Moraga Land Company which sold land to developers and subdivided the land. It established the town site of Moraga in 1913 and tried unsuccessfully to sell lots there. Slowly, however, it grew and, in 1974, was incorporated as the city of Moraga

MORENO VALLEY

162

Moreno Valley is not named exactly for a person named Moreno. It is named for a man named Brown. And "brown" means *moreno* in Spanish. In 1883 Frank E. Brown formed the Bear Valley Land and Water Company. He built a dam at Bear Valley in the San Bernardino Mountains and contracted to provide water to new communities of Moreno and Alessandro. Moreno was named for himself—more distinctive sounding than "Brown"--while Alessandro was named after the valley of that name where the towns were situated and was originally taken from the name of a character in the 1884 novel *Ramona* by Helen Hunt Jackson.

Brown was born in Connecticut and educated at Yale, graduating from the Sheffield Scientific School. After taking a post-graduate course in civil engineering at Yale, he left for California in 1877. Teaming with E. G. Judson, a young stockbroker from New York, they planned the "Red Lands Colony," helping build the California citrus industry. Judson and Brown helped establish an agriculturally based enterprise with the Washington navel orange thriving in the red adobe soil that had been sheep pastures. In 1984 the voters of Moreno, Edgemont, and Sunnymead joined together to form a new city, Moreno Valley.

Hiram Morgan Hill

MORGAN HILL

The Santa Clara Valley city takes its name not from the hill—called El Toro (used in its seal and logo)—that overlooks the city, but from Hiram Morgan Hill (1848-1913) who married into a pioneer family and in 1884 built an estate called *Villa Miramonte*, named for the view of the mountain. When the first Southern Pacific station was built in 1898, the railroad referred to the area as Huntington. Many visitors requested that the train stop at Morgan Hill's ranch, and soon the town's name was changed accordingly. Morgan Hill—he rarely used the Hiram—came to California from Missouri in the 1870s and met Diana Murphy while working at a bank in San Francisco. She was the daughter of cattle baron Daniel Murphy, the largest landowner in the world at that time. Diana was known as "The Duchess of Durango" for the vast ranching property her father owned in Mexico. Unfortunately, her father strongly disapproved of Hill, so they secretly married in 1882. Her father lay dying two months later and demanded that she never marry Hill. She agreed and after his death, she sought a divorce. However, before the case could be heard, her friends and family helped to reunite her with Hill. A year later, they left for a European honeymoon, then built *Villa Miramonte*. In 1892, the Hills divided their ranch property into 10- to 100-acre parcels and sold them to settlers lured to the development by national advertising. As people moved to the area, a small village called Morgan Hill began to grow around the stop. The Hills' marriage did not last; they separated and Hill left for the Nevada ranch that his wife had inherited where he spent his last years raising cattle.

MOSS LANDING

The little community on Monterey Bay was named for Charles Moss, a wealthy Texan and retired ship captain. He and a partner, after starting a line of schooners at the landing in 1865, constructed a 200-foot wharf to facilitate the loading of freight. It boomed with grain shipments, sardine canneries, whaling, and boat building, before its inevitable decline. He later sold his holdings to the Pacific Coast Steamship Company, but the town respected him enough to adopt his name. Unfortunately, the wharf and much of the town's infrastructure were destroyed by an earthquake in 1906. The wharf is today part of the **Moss Landing Harbor District**, the largest Special District in California.

MUIR WILDERNESS, JOHN

First designated for protection in 1964, the John Muir Wilderness in the Inyo and Sierra National Forests extends for over a 580,323 acres, It seems only proper that it is named for John Muir (1838-1914), inventor, immigrant, botanist, glaciologist, writer, co-founder of the Sierra Club, fruit rancher. But it was his love of nature, and the preservation of it, that he is best remembered. He convinced President Theodore Roosevelt to protect Yosemite, Sequoia, Grand Canyon and Mt. Rainier as National Parks. His home in Martinez is now the **John Muir National Historic Site**. **Muir Woods National Monument** is located just north of San Francisco in Marin County. **Mount Muir**, about a mile from Mount Whitney, at 14,015 feet, is the eleventh highest peak in California

MURPHYS

John Murphy (1825-1892) and his family were part of the 1844 Stephens-Townsend-Murphy party, the first to successfully bring wagons over the Sierra. He settled in San Jose. In 1846-47 he fought in the Mexican War. After his discharge, when he heard about gold being discovered, he wasted no time reaching the gold fields. In August or September of 1848, John opened a small trading post near Placerville. When the gold started to play out, Murphy headed south, settling in Calaveras County. With his brother Daniel, he opened up a trading post in an area that became known as Murphys Diggings. John, although only 23 years old, knew how to handle the local Indians. He was very successful in getting them to mine gold for him in trade for merchandise from his business. It was said that by the time he left Murphys in 1849, he had well over 2 million dollars in gold with him. Two years later a post office was established there. He returned to San Jose and the following year was elected Santa Clara County's first Treasurer. In 1854 he was elected to the San Jose City Council. He next served as Sheriff of Santa Clara County from 1857 to 1861, after which he devoted himself to business. Meanwhile back at Murphys Diggings, the name was changed to Murphy in 1894, then, in 1935, to Murphys.

MURRAY RANCH STATE PARK, BURLEIGH H.

Burleigh Hall Murray (1892-1978) was the grandson of Miranda Murray, the widow of Robert Mills who acquired 1,100 acres along the San Mateo coast near Half Moon Bay (most of this 1,325-acre park) between 1862 and 1884. Over the years, he developed his ranch and leased it to immigrant English, Irish, Italian, and Portuguese farmers. The property was passed through the family until the estate of Burleigh Hall Murray donated the ranch to the state of California in 1979 as a living monument to early San Mateo County ranch life.

MURRIETA

Iziquel Murietta came to the Temecula Valley and bought two *ranchos* totaling 52,000 acres for a dollar an acre. He had to go back to his native Spain to marry, so he turned his holdings over to his younger brother, Juan Murietta (1844-1936), who brought a flock of about 100,000 sheep to the valley in 1873. Some years later he sold all his land, but for 1000 of the choicest acres, each worth several hundred dollars. In 1886 he sold them as well and moved to Los Angeles where he raised avocados.

N

NEWBERRY SPRINGS

The little desert community due west of the Mojave
National Preserve takes its name from a one-time manager
of the local railroad station. Packages shipped to this area
carried a stamp with his name, "Newberry," on it to
designate which station it was to be left at for pickup. It
was in the 1950's that the Postal Service required the
community to add "Springs" to it's name in order to
distinguish it from Newbury Park.

NEWBURY PARK

The Ventura County Conejo Valley area (much of which
has been subsumed by the city of Thousand Oaks) is
named for its first postmaster, Egbert Starr Newbury
(1843-1880). Born in Michigan, after serving in the Union
Army in the Civil War, he came West for health reasons
and bought a large ranch in the valley—christened
"Newbury Park"--and two years later opened its first post
office. In 1877 he was financially ruined by a devastating
drought which forced him and his family to return to

Michigan where he died three years later of pneumonia.

NEWMAN
Simon Newman (1846-1912) immigrated to the United States from Bavaria when he was fifteen. In 1869 he came to Hill's Ferry on the west side of the San Joaquin Valley, where he opened a general store. With profits made in retailing, he bought large tracts of land in the 1870s, where he grew wheat and barley and raised sheep and cattle. When the Union Pacific extended its line down Stanislaus County's west side, he donated some of his land as a right-of-way. When the town of Newman was laid out on this land in 1887, the people of Hill's Ferry and those living at the German settlement of Dutch Corners, two miles away, were induced to move to the new town, leaving those communities as ghost towns. Newman prospered there, operating a store and a bank, owned grain elevators, rented land and made loans. The business was incorporated in 1889 as the Simon Newman Company and evolved into what one contemporary termed an "empire." Upon his retirement Newman moved to San Francisco.

NICOLAS, SAN
Vizcaíno sailed through the Santa Barbara Channel on December 6, 1602, the feast day of Saint Nicholas (270-346) and named one of the islands for the saint, who is also known as Nicholas of Myra, a city in Turkey. Because of his reputation for clandestine gifting—he would leave money in the shoes of those who put them out for him—Saint Nicholas is said to be the model for Santa Claus.

NOVATO
The northern Marin County city takes its name from the Mexican land grant *Rancho Novato,* which was named after a Coast Miwok chief who, it seems, was christened at his baptism as Novatus, after the second-century saint. Almost nothing is known of Saint Novatus, other than he was an early Roman convert to Christianity.

O

O'NEILL NATIONAL HISTORIC SITE, EUGENE

America's only Nobel Prize-winning playwright, Eugene O'Neill (1888-1953) and his wife Carlotta built Tao House near Danville and chose to live there at the climax of his writing career (1937-1944). Isolated from the world and within the walls of his home, the dramatist wrote his last six plays, including "A Moon for the Misbegotten," "The Iceman Cometh," and "Long Day's Journey Into Night." In 1976 the property became a national historic site.

ONOFRE STATE BEACH, SAN

The San Diego County beach was most likely named by the Spanish *padres* on June 12, the feast day of San Onofre, the Spanish name of Saint Onuphrius Magnus (c. 330-c. 400), who lived in the Egyptian desert as a hermit, existing on the fruits of a date-palm tree that grew near his cell. He wore no clothes. He was later adopted in the West as the patron of weavers.

ORCUTT

The Santa Maria suburb dozed through the last quarter of the nineteenth century until it was revived by an oil boom in 1904. The town was renamed in honor of William Orcutt (1869- 1942) a Union Oil geologist and civil engineer who worked in the Santa Maria Valley as the company's district manager. Orcutt grew up in Santa Paula where as a youth he sometimes worked at odd jobs at the Union Oil refinery before entering Stanford to study engineering and geology. One of the college's first four-year graduates, he was a member of the pioneer class of 1895. Hired by Union Oil in 1899, Orcutt was soon running the geology program. He made the first geology maps of many of California's most important oil fields. A gifted explorer, he developed a staff of top-flight oil finders and built a reputation as the dean of West Coast petroleum geologists. In 1901 Orcutt was intrigued by the La Brea tar pits just west of Los Angeles. He found evidence of a scientific treasure house --"a mosaic of white bones, uniform in shape, lying in an exact pattern...a beautiful contrast with the black surface of the hard asphaltum." Orcutt kept his discovery quiet to save the tar pits from "relic hunters," eventually contacting the University of California in Berkeley who confirmed the find in 1906. Thereafter, scientists from many universities and museums were digging through the "muck" to recover thousands of bones of prehistoric animals. In 1908 Orcutt became Union Oil's chief geologist, land department manager and a company director. In 1922 he was named vice president of the company. Part of his retirement estate in Canoga Park now constitutes the **Orcutt Ranch Horticultural Center**.

ORD DUNES STATE PARK, FORT

The former army post on Monterey Bay is named for Major General Edward O. C. Ord (1818-1883). He served in the army, from the date of his graduation from West Point in 1839 to his retirement in 1881, at various posts from California to Florida. At the start of the Civil War he served in the Western Theater of Operation and was

170

wounded at the battle of Hatchie, Mississippi. A corps commander during the battle of Vicksburg, Ord served in Louisiana and the Shenandoah Valley before joining federal forces at Petersburg. Wounded again in 1864, it was Ord's forced march from Farmville to Appomattox that ended the Army of Northern Virginia's chances to escape to the Blue Ridge Mountains.

ORINDA

There are two theories as to how the Contra Costa city got its name. One is that it is named for Martin Orinda, a renowned Spanish architect of the seventeenth century. The more likely theory is that its name came courtesy of Alice Marsh Cameron. Apparently in 1876 she named a tract of land owned by her husband after an obscure seventeenth century English poet, Katherine Phillips (1631-1666), who used "Orinda" as her *nom de plume*, and was known in her circle as the "Matchless Orinda." Cameron called the tract "Orinda Park" but the "Park" was subsequently dropped.

OWENS VALLEY

In 1845 John C. Frémont named **Owens Lake** for Richard ("Dick") Owens (1812-1902), one of his guides. The river and valley take their names from the lake as does Owens Peak and Owens Peak Wilderness.. The Owens Valley was considered a great thoroughfare for travel to and from the Nevada mining districts of Esmeralda and Washoe, the Great Salt Lake in Utah, and southern California. It was also considered a significant military route for supplies and communications to and from California. Owens himself never saw the area.

The Baltimore-born Owens was described by Edwin Legrand Sabin in his *Kit Carson Days* (1914) as "Carson's close comrade and partner in many mountain doings; his partner in ranching it in New Mexico after trapper days; his companion upon the third Frémont expedition, and captain in California service during the events which followed the Bear Flag. A man 'cool, brave and of good judgment.'"

Henry Oxnard

OXNARD

Encouraged by a pledge of 18,000 acres of sugar beets from local farmers, in 1897 Henry T. Oxnard (1860-1922), head of the American Beet Sugar Factories in California and Nebraska, constructed a two million dollar factory in Ventura County. A town quickly sprang up nearby and soon homes and businesses appeared around the town square. By 1903, it was large enough to incorporate as the "City of Oxnard," though, so the story goes, its namesake wanted to name it for the Greek word for "sugar—*Zachari*, but frustrated by bureaucratic entanglement, named it for himself. Henry Oxnard grew up in Brooklyn and attended Harvard. His various beet sugar factories were consolidated in 1890 as the American Beet Sugar Company, of which he was the first president. In 1906 he retired, moving to New York City, and turning the company over to his brother Robert.

P

PABLO, SAN

The name San Pablo was given to the land in 1811 by Ramón Abella, a priest from Mission Dolores in San Francisco, which was using the land on the opposite coast of the San Francisco Bay ("contra costa") to raise food for the mission. He named the two points opposite each other on the bay "Point San Pablo" and "Point San Pedro." Saint Paul (c. 5 BC-67AD) was the foremost early Christian missionary. *Rancho San Pablo* was a 17,939-acre land grant given, upon Mexico's independence from Spain in 1823, by Governor Arguello to Francisco María Castro (1775-1831), a former soldier at the San Francisco Presidio and one-time *alcalde* of the Pueblo of San José.. The. grant covered what is now Richmond, San Pablo, and Kensington in Contra Costa County and was given the name *Rancho San Pablo*, thus originating the name for today's city, incorporated in 1948. **San Pablo Bay** is an estuary that forms the northern part of San Francisco Bay.

PACHECO VALLEY

The Contra Costa County valley is named for Don Salvio Pacheco (1793-1876). In 1834 he was given an 18,000-acre land grant called *Rancho Monte del Diablo* and in the 1840s completed a two-story adobe, the first building to be erected in the valley. Pacheco gave the land surrounding this adobe to the refugees of the earthquake-flood of 1868, and the community became known as Concord

PACHECO STATE PARK

The park is the last remaining portion of the 48,000-acre Mexican land grant *El Rancho San Luis Gonzaga* owned by Francisco Pacheco (1790-1860) and his son Juan (1823-1855) who built the first house in Merced County on it in 1843. After Spanish rule ended and the Mexican era began, Francisco Pacheco became one of the wealthiest land owners of California. Born in Guadalajara, Mexico, he arrived in Monterey as a poor wagon maker. Through hard work his real estate holdings eventually extended from Gilroy to San Juan Bautista to parts of the pass. People began calling the pass "Pacheco" after him. The *rancho* stayed in the family for a century. Paula Fatjo, a San Francisco debutante and fifth generation descendant of the Pachecos, moved into the adobe fort-turned-ranch headquarters in 1948. She desired to live the life of a rustic *ranchero* in emulation of her nineteenth-century relatives. Unfortunately for her bucolic way of life, the state of California began construction of the mammoth San Luis Reservoir and she was forced to sell her soon-to-be-underwater ranch to the state in 1963. She then relocated her ranch, historic adobe and all, twelve miles west to the top of **Pacheco Pass**.

PARDEE DAM

The dam, reservoir and lake in Amador County are all named for George Pardee (1857-1941). Born in San Francisco and raised in Oakland, after graduating from the University of California he went on to medical school, and eventually practiced medicine in Oakland. He served on the Board of Health, the Oakland City Council, and eventually as Mayor. In 1903 he successfully ran for Governor. He was an important Progressive Era voice in California Republican politics, but his efforts at reform during his governorship brought on the wrath of the railroads and lost him the nomination of his party for a second term. He went on to work for conservationist causes and, as president of the East Bay Municipal Utilities District, helped bring Mokelumne River water to Oakland. For those efforts the Pardee Dam on that river was named after him.

PARLIER
The San Joaquin Valley town is named for I.N. Parlier (1842-1916) who arrived in 1876 from Springfield, Illinois. He opened the General Store and Trading Post that became the Fresno County community's first post office in 1898.

PASQUAL VALLEY, SAN
The name of the valley east of Escondido in San Diego County derives from an early Native American pueblo of that name which was given to it by the Franciscans at Mission San Diego. The original "San Pascual" morphed into "San Pasqual"—a spelling used in Army reports after the famous battle there. **San Pasqual Battlefield State Historic Park** honors the soldiers who fought in the clash between the U.S. and *Californio* forces on December 6, 1846 in the midst of the Mexican-American War. Generals Stephen Kearny and Andres Pico both claimed victory. The battle was only one of the military encounters in California in the war, but it proved to be the bloodiest and most controversial as to the outcome Saint Paschal (1540-1592) was a Spanish lay brother of the Franciscan order known for his charity to the afflicted and poor.

PATRICK'S POINT STATE PARK
There are conflicting views as for whom the coastal redwood park near Trinidad in Mendocino County is named. One holds that its namesake is Patrick Beegan (or Beagan), an Irish immigrant who came to the area via the

Mississippi Valley and homesteaded the headland in 1851, though other accounts state that he had come to prospect for gold, but decided to build a trading post instead He was a trader and had earlier worked with the U.S. Army as a scout during the Indian wars and was ultimately killed by a group of Chilula Indians in the 1860s.

The other Patrick, Patrick McLaughlin, did not come to the area until the 1870s and squatted on the logged-over property that now makes up the park. The name Patrick's Point was first shown on the county map of 1886, a late date that favors the McLaughlin theory.

The park was established in 1930 to protect a wooded region and coastal rock formations and has an area of 640 acres.

PATTERSON

Born in upstate New York, Thomas W. Patterson (1859-1914) moved to Fresno in 1888 where his uncle John Patterson had settled. He got into the real estate and lending business before joining the Fresno National Bank in 1896, becoming its president four years later. In 1902 he inherited an interest in over 18,000 acres of land in Stanislaus County from his Uncle John, which the latter had acquired in 1866, part of the *Rancho Del Puerto* grant. Thomas and his brother, William, bought out the other heirs for $540,000 in cash and incorporated the Patterson Ranch Company in 1908. They subdivided the land into ranches of various sizes and plotted the design of the town of Patterson. Determined to make it different from other cities, they modeled it after Washington D.C. and Paris, using a series of circles and radiating streets. It is today known as the "Apricot Capital of the World."

PAULA, SANTA

Situated in the Santa Clara River Valley of Ventura County, the city was originally part of the *Rancho Santa Paula y Saticoy*, a Mexican land grant of 1843. Part of it was bought in 1872 by N. W. Blanchard who founded the town.

Saint Paula (347-404) was thirty-two years old, a wealthy mother of five, when her husband died. A close

176

friendship with Saint Jerome helped her cope with her grief and resulted in a newfound religious devotion. She left her home and made a pilgrimage with one of her daughters to join Saint Jerome in Bethlehem where she remained until her death.

PEDRO, SAN

Vizcaíno entered San Pedro Bay, Los Angeles' port of entry, in 1602 and named it for Saint Peter, Bishop of Alexandria, whose feast day it was. A native of the Egyptian city, he survived the persecutions of Emperor Diocletian and served as a confessor for the suffering Christians. He composed a set of rules by which those who had lapsed might be readmitted to the faith after appropriate penance, a settlement which was not to the liking of extremists of the community. Thus, in 306 when the persecutions began again, Peter was forced to flee the city, returning five years later after a lull in the persecutions, but was soon arrested and beheaded by Roman officials acting on the decree of Emperor Maximian. He is called the "seal and complement of martyrs" as he was the last Christian slain by Roman authorities.

PENDLETON, CAMP

The 200-square-mile Marine facility in San Diego County is named for Major General Joseph Henry Pendleton (1860-1942) who during his forty-six years of service in the Corps (1878-1924) pioneered its services in southern California. A graduate of the Naval Academy, he saw service in the Spanish-American War in Cuba and the Philippines. He became enamored of the San Diego area when his regiment was sent there in 1914 and promoted it as an ideal choice for a Marine Corps base. After his retirement in 1924, he lived in Coronado and became active in civic affairs, serving as mayor from 1929 to 1930. Within two months of his death in 1942 construction started of a base on the former *Rancho Santa Margarita y Las Flores* near Oceanside that would bear his name.

PENN VALLEY

It is supposed that the Nevada County community is named for one Madame Penn. She was described by a contemporary historian: "For a number of years ladies, especially of a desirable kind, were in a woeful minority, but now their sweet presence and refining influence are a power in the city for good. Madame Penn came in the fall of 1849; she was an indefatigable worker, taking her turn with [her miner] husband in carrying dirt and agitating the rocker." She opened a boarding house and prospered, eventually owning a 320-acre homestead at the intersection of the colorfully named Grub Creek and Squirrel Creek. She sold it to a gold miner in 1852 who enlarged the property, which, in time, became present-day Penn Valley.

PERRIS

Before the 1880's the Perris Valley in southwest Riverside County was known as the San Jacinto Plains after the river that crosses it. In 1881 the California Southern Railroad decided to lay their tracks through the valley, thereby terminating the transcontinental route of the Santa Fe Railway at San Diego. Fredrick Thomas Perris (1837-1916) was put in personal charge of all surveying and construction of the route. With the completion of the railroad, settlers began flocking to the valley in the early 1880s, staking out homesteads and buying railroad land at a new town site to be called Perris. It was officially named a station of the Santa Fe in 1886. In 1911 Perris became an incorporated city. **Lake Perris** is an artificial lake constructed in 1973 and is now part of the **Lake Perris State Recreation Area**.

PFEIFFER BEACH

Michael Pfeiffer (1832-1917) was an 1869 homesteader in the Big Sur Valley; **Pfeiffer Big Sur State Park** is named for his son John, (1862-1941) and **Julia Pfeiffer Burns State Park** for his daughter Julia (1868-1928). She was close to her parents and stayed on at their home on Pfeiffer Beach to take care of them in their old age. In 1915 she married John Burns, a Scottish orphan who lived with the nearby Post family. They continued to live and ranch in the Big Sur country until her death. Michael Pfeiffer had come to Big Sur in 1869 with his sixteen-year-old wife, Barbara. They built a house near the mouth of Sycamore Canyon in 1869. There son John homesteaded a 160-acre parcel on the north bank of the Big Sur River and in 1884 moved to the site of the Homestead Cabin. When Big Sur became more popular and the need for accommodations became apparent, John and his wife, Florence, opened Pfeiffer's Ranch Resort on the site of today's Big Sur Lodge. In 1933 the State of California purchased 680 acres of land from John Pfeiffer and named the new park in his honor.

In the 1920s former New York Congressman Lathrop Brown and his wife, Helen, bought Saddle Rock Ranch. In 1961 Helen donated it to the state park system, with the proviso that it be named in honor of her friend and Big Sur pioneer Julia Pfeiffer.

PICO RIVERA

Founded in 1784 it was not incorporated until 1958 when the long-standing unincorporated communities of Pico (named for Pío Pico [1801-1894], the last Mexican governor of California) and Rivera ("brook" or "stream" in Spanish), probably from where the Rio Hondo and San Gabriel Rivers merged. Pico, the grandson of one of the soldiers that accompanied de Anza on his expedition to California in 1775, started off as a merchant in Los Angeles and soon became one of the richest men in Alta California. In 1850 he bought the 9,000-acre *Rancho Paso de Bartolo* (which included half of present-day Whittier) and built a home on it, now preserved as **Pio Pico State Historic Park**. He was twice Governor of Alta California (1832 and 1845). During the Mexican-American War, when U.S. troops occupied Los Angeles and San Diego in 1846, Pico fled to Baja California to argue the case for sending troops to defend California before the Mexican Congress as well as prevent himself being taken prisoner. After the war, Pico returned to Los Angeles, successfully surviving the Mexican-American transition and in 1853 was elected mayor. He returned to his businesses, but because of gambling losses and unwise business decisions, he had to liquidate his holdings and spent his last years impoverished.

PITTSBURG
The city at the junction of the San Joaquin and Sacramento Rivers in Contra Costa County was originally known as New York Landing, but in 1911, a few years after Columbia Geneva Steel opened for business, the name was changed by popular vote to Pittsburg, after the eastern capital of the steel industry, but without the "H" for simplified spelling. The Pennsylvania city was named in honor of the English statesman William Pitt (1708-1778).

PIXLEY
Frank Morrison Pixley (1825-1895), a New Yorker, a lawyer by profession, came to California with a wagon train when he was twenty-four, After a year of unsuccessful mining, he came to San Francisco to practice law, where in 1852, he was elected City Attorney. He acted as State Attorney General in 1862 and 1863, as well as a University of California Regent (1875-1880). He invested in farming land he owned in Tulare County which named the agricultural community in what is now the Visalia-Porterville metro area for him in 1886. In 1877, when he was fifty-three, a new career opened up when he founded the San Francisco Argonaut, which he published and edited until his death in 1895 and continued until 1958.

Alfred Pleasonton

PLEASANTON

The Alameda County city is named for Civil War General Alfred Pleasonton (1824-1897), and misspelled by a recording clerk at the Washington, D.C. registration office to become "Pleasanton." A West Point graduate, Pleasonton fought throughout the War with Mexico (1846-1848), and in numerous Indian battles. During the opening months of the Civil War he was a member of the U.S. Dragoons which was consolidated into the U.S. Cavalry in August 1861. He fought throughout the Peninsular Campaign and was promoted from major to brigadier general of volunteers. Subsequently, he was in combat during the battles of South Mountain, Antietam, and Fredericksburg.

. After the war, as part of the general reduction of all officers' ranks, Pleasonton reverted to major and, dissatisfied with his command relationship to former subordinates, resigned his commission in 1868. As a civilian, he worked as U.S. Collector of Internal Revenue, but he was asked to resign after he lobbied Congress for the repeal of the income tax. Refusing to resign, he was dismissed. He served briefly as the president of the Terre Haute and Cincinnati Railroad.

POLLOCK PINES

The unincorporated area in El Dorado County is named

181

for Hiram R. Pollock (1865-1949) who migrated to the area at the turn of the twentieth century from Michigan. He was able to accumulate more than 6000 acres of land from which he harvested lumber. When his trees were wiped out by fire he decided to subdivide the land and sell lots for $5 down and $5 per month. He called the development Pollock Pines.

PORTER RANCH
The planned community in the northwest corner of the San Fernando Valley was constructed by the Porter Ranch Development Company. In 1869 the former San Fernando Mission lands were divided in half, with the northern half of the valley being sold to Charles Maclay and George Keating Porter (1833-1906). Porter then sold part of his land to his cousin, Benjamin Franklin Porter. Maclay planned to build a town on his share of the land, which later became the city of San Fernando. The Porter cousins planned to plant crops and raised cattle. Their original ranch is the core of the today's community. George K. Porter came to California in 1849 from Massachusetts, working as a miner, lumberman, and farmer. With his cousin he established a successful leather manufacturing firm in San Francisco and set out buying large parcels of land throughout the state, including the San Fernando property.

PORTERVILLE
Originally settled by gold prospectors, Porterville was named after Royal Porter Putnam (1837-1889) who came to the area from Pennsylvania in 1858 to manage the Tule River stagecoach station, which was eventually called Porter Station. With the region's growing farm and ranch enterprises, Putnam bought forty acres of land and built a hotel and store helping to create the community that would be named for him. His middle name was used because another Putnam family lived south of town.

PORTOLA
In 1910 Virgilia Bogue, queen of the 1909 Portola Festival

182

in San Francisco and daughter of Virgil Bogue, a prominent local engineer for the Western Pacific (the main railway through the region) suggested in passing that the Plumas County town be named Portola, and soon thereafter, at a town meeting, it became official.

Gaspar de Portolá [(1716-1784) found San Francisco Bay that was missed earlier by Vizcaíno. He served in the Spanish army in Italy and Portugal before serving as Governor of Baja California from 1768-1770. In 1768, he volunteered to lead an expedition being planned to create bases up the California coast in San Diego and Monterey. The San Mateo County city of **Portola Valley** is also named for the explorer, as is **Portola Redwoods State Park** on the western slopes of the Santa Cruz Mountains.

Q

QUENTIN, SAN

The small Marin County community and the notorious prison across from it take their name from Point San Quentin on the San Francisco Bay. There is no saint named Quentin, however; rather, it is an intentional change from the original *Punta de Quintin*, named for a sub-chief of Chief Marin, for whom the county is named. General Vallejo wrote, in 1874, that it was "reserved from the North Americans to change the name of that place, and to call it 'Punta de San Quentin.' I believe that the change may be attributed to the fact that large numbers of them arrived in California under the belief that the inhabitants of this country were very zealous Catholics, and desiring to gain their good-will added *San* (Saint) before the towns or villages that they visited. I remember having heard on different occasions 'Santa Sonoma," "San Branciforte," and 'San Monterey," and, pursuant to this custom, they added San to Quentin."

QUINCY

The town was originally called American Ranch (1850-1854). It became Quincy around the time it was chosen as the county seat of the newly-formed Plumas County on March 18, 1854. The owner of the ranch, Hugh J. Bradley, offered to donate some of his land for a new courthouse if the town name were changed to honor his hometown of Quincy, Illinois. The latter was named in 1825 for the newly-elected President of the United States, John Quincy Adams.

R

RAFAEL, SAN

Marin County's seat began with the founding of the *Misión San Rafael Arcángel* in 1817. As the mortality rate of the native Americans at Mission Dolores in San Francisco had risen alarmingly, the *padres* decided to build a kind of *rancho* with chapel, baptistery, and cemetery across the Golden Gate. The name San Rafael Arcángel was selected so the angel "who in his name expresses 'the healing of God' might care for bodies as well as souls."

RAMON, SAN

In 1797 what would be the city of San Ramon was San Jose Mission grazing land. Later it was included in José María Amador's 16,000-acre *Rancho San Ramón*, which took its name from **San Ramon Creek**, named after an Indian *vaquero* called Ramón, who tended mission sheep there. The area around it was known as the **San Ramon Valley** In an 1855 land title case, Don Amador explained that "San" was added to the creek's name to conform with Spanish custom. It was incorporated in 1983.

REDDING

Situated in the northern Sacramento Valley, the city's genesis is the land granted in 1846 by Mexico to Maj. Pearson B. Reading, the 25,000-acre *Rancho Buenaventura*. When the Central Pacific Railroad came to Shasta County in 1872 it founded the town and named it after its land agent, Benjamin B. Redding (1824-1882), rather than Major Reading. This did not sit well with the locals. In 1874 its representative in the California Assembly introduced a bill changing the name to Reading. For six years it was known by that name, but rail officials refused to make the change. To avoid confusion, in 1880 the Assembly repealed the earlier bill and it was rechristened as Redding.

Before being land agent, the Nova Scotia-born Redding moved to Boston when he was sixteen, and lighted out for the West in 1849 as part of the Gold Rush. He was successful in mining ventures and business enterprises and was in the State Assembly (1853-54) when the capital was in Benecia. He served as mayor of Sacramento (1856), was the first Secretary of State (1863-67), and, in later years, took a great interest in horticulture, the preservation of game and the propagation of fish. He was also a University of California Regent in the 1880s and the first president of the Fish Commission of California, an office he held at the time of his death

REEDLEY

Civil war veteran Thomas Law Reed (1847-1911) had come to California in 1876, farming first in Yolo County, then, in 1884, moving to what was then known as Smith's Ferry in Fresno County. Popular accounts say that he came with eleven head of horses and mules, and $1,000 of borrowed money There he began a steady expansion of his farming operation. In 1888 the Southern Pacific Railroad was building a branch line through the area heading south to Porterville. Reed deeded a half-interest in a 360-acre town site to the Pacific Improvement Company, a

Southern Pacific subsidiary, and in return they established a depot. This new town needed a name, and the railroad determined that it should be "Reedley." Soon, buildings and streets grew amid the wheat fields that paralleled the railroad tracks. Reed built and owned the town's first hotel, livery stable and blacksmith forge.

RICHARDSON BAY

On August 22, 1822 the *Orion,* an English whaler, put into Yerba Buena Cove for supplies. On it was Captain William A. Richardson (1795-1856), a Liverpuddlian described as "tall, fair-haired, blue-eyed and young." The Mexican authorities allowed him to stay ashore on condition that he teach navigation and carpentry to the young Californians. He soon established a base near San Gabriel in southern California and traded up and down the coast as far south as Peru, making his reputation as a navigator and pilot. In 1835 he returned to San Francisco Bay and was the first inhabitant of Yerba Buena, where he erected the first building in the town. He was Captain of the Port and also dealt privately in hides and tallow collected from area ranches. He married the daughter of a Mexican officer of the Presidio and bought a large ranch covering the present site of Sausalito, where he lived for many years. In 1856, ailing and in financial straits, Richardson put *Rancho Saucelito* into the hands of an administrator, Samuel P. Throckmorton, and died two months later. Part of San Francisco Bay, Richardson Bay, was later named for him.

Friend Richardson

RICHARDSON GROVE STATE PARK "The Grove," located in southern Humboldt County, started in 1922 with 120 acres and has grown to over 2,000. It was named after Friend W. Richardson (1865-1943) who served as State Treasurer (1915-1923) before being elected Governor (1923-1927). Born in a Quaker colony in Michigan as William Richardson, he moved with his family at an early age to San Bernardino. He legally changed his name to the Quaker greeting "Friend." His Quaker beliefs would not allow his family to have servants at the Governor's Mansion. He ran a "no-frills" administration, frequently vetoing measures that would increase spending. He even felt that education had become too costly and tried (but failed) to close two colleges. His efforts left a $20 million surplus in the state treasury. In the 1930s he served as State Building and Loan Commissioner and, later, as the State Superintendent of Banks.

RIPLEY DESERT WOODLAND STATE, PARK ARTHUR B.

Arthur Ripley (1901-1989) was a turkey farmer in western Antelope Valley who provided in his will that 565 acres of Joshua and juniper trees on his property go to the state of California to be maintained as a park. He had never cultivated that woodland area, believing that it one day

189

should be preserved in its natural state. The park opened in 1990.

ROBERTS, CAMP

Construction of the camp along Highway 101 near San Miguel began in 1940 and was first known as Camp Nacimiento Replacement Training Center. It was changed to Camp Roberts in honor of a San Francisco native Corp. Harold W. Roberts (1895-1916), a tank driver in World War I. His tank fell into a crater filled with rainwater while maneuvering to aid another tank. While the tank rapidly filled with water, Corporal Roberts shoved the gunner out, but was unable to get himself out and drowned. For his selfless act, he was awarded the Medal of Honor posthumously. In seeking an appropriate name twenty-two years later for a camp with a primary purpose of training new soldiers, the Army remembered Roberts, who was only 19 years old when he died. Camp Roberts is one of only a few military posts named for an enlisted man.

ROGERS STATE HISTORIC PARK, WILL

During the 1930s, the Oklahoma-born "Cowboy-Philosopher" (1879-1935) was among the most popular and highest paid actors in Hollywood. From his start in vaudeville with a trick roping act, he rose to fame as a columnist, philosopher, radio personality, and movie star. In 1922 he bought land in Santa Monica, where he developed a ranch. Eventually, he owned 186 acres overlooking the Pacific Ocean, in what is now Pacific Palisades. At his untimely death in a plane crash, the ranch consisted of a 31-room ranch house, a stable, corrals, riding ring, roping arena, polo field, golf course, and hiking trails. When his widow, Betty, died in 1944, the ranch became a state park. **Will Rogers State Beach** is nearby.

ROHNERT PARK

The Sonoma County town is named after the family who owned the Rohnert Seed Farm. Waldo Emerson Rohnert (1869-1933) of Detroit had come to California and joined with the C.C. Morse Company, the largest seed growing firm in the west. In 1893 he started his own business in Hollister, where he also planted one of the largest prune orchards in the country. He then expanded into the San Joaquin Valley then, in 1929, moved north to Cotati. After his death, his son Fred took over the ranch and turned the Rohnert Seed Farm into a major success. The city that grew around it became Rohnert Park.

ROSA, SANTA

The first deeded land in this section of Sonoma County was held as the *Rancho Cabeza de Santa Rosa*. According to popular legend, it was named Santa Rosa by Father Juan Amorosa. After baptizing a young Native American woman in a stream, he followed the usual custom of naming rivers and creeks for saints. Because the baptism took place on the day of the Feast of Santa Rosa de Lima (1586-1617), her name was given to the stream (and later to the whole valley) as well as to the young woman who was baptized. Saint Rose was born in Lima, Peru where at twenty she became a Dominican nun, known for the variety and severity of her penances, including the constant wearing of a metal spiked crown concealed by roses. She was the first American to be canonized.

Santa Rosa is also the name of one of the Channel Islands.

ROSAMOND

Just who Rosamond was will probably never be known. Like many California settlements this Antelope Valley town started off as a train stop. As owners of the site, the Santa Fe Railroad got to name it whatever it wanted, in this case (in 1877) one of its officials named it for his daughter. What his name was and what became of the fair Rosamond are lost to history.

ROSS

The Marin County town was named in honor of Scottish immigrant James Ross (1812-1862), who purchased the land in 1857 for $50,000. He had arrived in California by way of Tasmania and like many a '49er made his money not from mining but by selling miners with supplies and spirits. He became a wealthy liquor dealer in San Francisco and built his "country estate" in Marin County. When he died, his wife, Ann, was forced to sell a portion of his larger land holdings to pay each of their daughters $10,000 as stipulated in his will. She retained 297 acres. When the North Pacific Coast Railroad inched its way upcounty in 1873, it named the stop between Larkspur and San Anselmo "Sunnyside." But when the area's growing population made it necessary to upgrade the stop to a full-fledged train station, Ann donated 1.4 acres to the cause—provided the station (and, by extension, the settlement) be renamed in honor of her late husband. It became official in 1908 when the town of Ross was officially incorporated.

ROWLAND HEIGHTS

John Rowland (1791-1873) came from England to America with his parents, settling in Boston. He decided to try his luck as a fur trapper and went west where he was hired on in Taos, New Mexico. In 1841 he and a friend, William Workman, led a group of a few dozen settlers to California's San Gabriel Valley—in what appears to be the first documented immigrant wagon train. Almost immediately they discovered that an almost 50,000-acre parcel of land—*Rancho La Puente*—was available. They were able to convince the Mexican authorities that they should receive the grant. Both Rowland and Workman built large homes there and soon were running a successful stock-raising and wheat-growing business. They also grew grapes and produced wine. In 1851, they decided to split their property, with Rowland taking about 29,000 acres on the east and Workman receiving the 20,000 acres on the west. Rowland became the state's first large-scale commercial winemaker. At his death, his estate passed to his heirs. Rowland Heights was comprised mostly of orange groves until affordable housing was built attracting families from Los Angeles.

RUBIDOUX

The Riverside County community's name stems from an

early California settler Louis Rubidoux (1796-1868). Born in St. Louis of French-Canadian parents, he is supposed to have won $30,000 at cards in Santa Fe which supplied the capital for his move in 1844 to California where he established an orchard, a large livestock operation, and the area's first grist mill. In 1860 he was the highest paying tax payer in the state. He served as a judge and a county supervisor.

RUSSELL, MOUNT

California's seventh highest peak (14,094 feet), less than a mile from Mount Whitney, is named for Israel Cook Russell (1852- 1906), a geologist best known for his explorations in Alaska. Writer and teacher in the fields of geology and geography, he did research in Mono Lake and Mount Lyell regions of California.

RUTHERFORD

The historic grape growing center of the Napa Valley stretches south of its central location to Yountville, where George Yount settled in 1838. He had three granddaughters, one of whom, Elizabeth, married Thomas Lewis Rutherford (1834-1892) in 1864. As a wedding present, the newlyweds received 1,040 acres at the northern end of Yount's land grant, *Rancho Caymus*. While Yount is considered to be the first to plant wine grapes in Napa Valley, it was Rutherford who made a serious investment in grape production and winemaking. From 1850 to 1880, he established himself as a grower of quality wines, though he seemed to have resided in San Francisco where he was in the flour business.

S

SANGER

The Fresno County city quickened into life in 1887 when the Southern Pacific Railroad began construction of a line from Fresno across eastern Fresno County and then south to Porterville. A few miles east of Fresno a depot was built called Sanger Junction after Joseph Sanger, Jr. (1832-1899), secretary-treasurer of the national Railroad Yardmaster's Association. Lots were auctioned off and soon settlers began to arrive. Shortly, Sanger Junction was shortened to Sanger. Joseph Sanger, born and raised in Watertown, Massachusetts, moved to Indiana as a young man to begin a career in railroading. He never visited the town named for him.

SANTEE

The Spanish parceled this region into land grants and divided them among Spanish soldiers in payment for services rendered. Years later, the land was sold to American settlers. George Cowles bought 4,000 acres in 1877 to develop his vineyards. The community became known as Cowlestown. Two years after his death in 1887, his widow, Jennie, married Milton Santee (1835-1927), a real-estate investor and civil engineer. In 1891 she was given permission to operate Cowlestown's post office under the name of her new husband. In 1893 the citizens of Cowlestown voted to follow suit and, in doing so, created the township which would become the city of Santee.

Milton Santee came from Missouri to Los Angeles in the 1880's where he became influential, serving on the city council from 1884-1886. He moved to San Diego to participate in a scheme, along with a number of other investors, to develop Coronado as a resort community. Unsuccessful in their first efforts, the investment group purchased some 3,800 acres in *Rancho Santa Maria* and formed the Santa Maria Land and Water Company. Within that acreage Santee surveyed and laid out the township of Nuevo, the name of which would later be changed (at Santee's suggestion) to Ramona.

SCOTTS VALLEY

The northern Santa Cruz County town is named for Hiram Scott (1823-1886) who bought the 4500-acre *Rancho San Agustín* in 1850 for $20,000. The son of a sea captain, Scott was a native of Maine who had jumped ship at Monterey in 1846 and ended up in Santa Cruz, where he worked on building ships. When word of the discovery of gold reached town, he headed for the Sierra where he set up a ferry service to bridge the San Joaquin River to the mining camps. In 1850 he opened the Stockton House, Stockton's first hotel. Scott returned to Scotts Valley in 1852 where he built Scott House on his newly-purchased land. During the following few years he sent for his large family in Maine to join him and soon the valley was inhabited solely by the Scotts and became known as Scotts Valley. In 1874 Hiram Scott moved to Arizona to try mining again, remaining there to prospect and farm until his death. In 1963 when the City of Santa Cruz went forward with plans to annex Scotts Valley, its residents countered by filing papers for incorporation, officially becoming a city in 1966.

SELMA
Local legend has it that the Fresno County town was named in 1880 after Selma Gruenberg Lewis (ca. 1867-1944) by Leland Stanford, head of the Central Pacific Railroad, who was shown her picture by her father. Stanford, the story goes, was so taken by her charm that he ordered the next town on the line be named "Selma." Lewis told the tale so often that it became accepted as true, though in fact, there was no real evidence. Later research showed that the little community was actually named for Selma Michelsen Kingsbury Latimer (1853-1910), wife of an assistant of the General Superintendent of the Central Pacific, who had submitted her name for inclusion on a list of candidate names prepared by his supervisor.

SEPULVEDA DAM
Sepulveda Dam is a flood control project constructed and operated by the U. S. Army Corps of Engineers in Los Angeles. It was opened in 1941. Behind the dam is the **Sepulveda Basin**, home of the **Sepulveda Basin Wildlife Refuge** and other parks. The **Sepulveda Pass** runs through the Santa Monica Mountains connecting the Los Angeles Basin to the San Fernando Valley. The community of Sepulveda in the San Fernando Valley changed its name to North Hills in 1992. It was named for Fernando Domingo Sepulveda (1814-1876), a grandson of the patriarch of the family, Francisco Xavier Sepulveda. Fernando acquired an interest in *Rancho San Rafael* in 1831, a 36,000-acre Spanish land grant owned by his father-in-law, José María Verdugo,

SERRA PEAK, JUNIPERO
The highest mountain of the Santa Lucia Range is named for the Franciscan priest who founded the California missions, Junípero Serra (1713-1784). Born in Mallorca, Spain, after taking holy orders he was sent to Mexico where he spent twenty years as a missionary. He was then appointed superior of a band of fifteen Franciscans for the Indian Missions of Baja California. He accompanied Portolá's land expedition to Alta California, founding the

first of the California missions at San Diego. The peak was originally named Santa Lucia Peak, but wanting to honor Serra, the Native Daughters of the Golden West had earlier bestowed his name upon a Sierra Nevada peak in 1905. However, the Sierra Club recommended that the name be transferred to Santa Lucia Peak. The United States Board on Geographic Names officially approved the name change the following year, finding that Serra was familiar with the Santa Lucia Mountains, though in fact it is doubtful that he ever encountered them.

SHAFTER

The Kern County town is named for William Rufus ("Pecos Bill") Shafter (1835-1906), the commanding general of American forces in Cuba during the Spanish-American War in 1898, the year the railroad was completed in the area and a siding was named in his honor. A large man in character and in size, he was born near Galesburg, Michigan, and had only a rudimentary education. During the Civil War he rose from private to major and won the Congressional Medal of Honor at the Battle of Fair Oaks (1862). After the war he was commissioned a lieutenant colonel and was sent to Texas where he commanded the all-black Twenty-fourth United States Infantry along the Rio Grande and earned the nickname of "Pecos Bill." He served primarily as a field commander which he was able to carry out despite his imposing physical bulk which would have slowed most officers. In 1897 he was promoted to brigadier general and led troops to Cuba during the Spanish American War (where he commanded Theodore Roosevelt), at which time he weighed over three hundred pounds and suffered from gout. Shortly after his promotion to major general in 1901, he retired to his sixty-acre farm adjoining his daughter's ranch in southwest Kern County, where he resided until his death.

SHAVER LAKE

The lake in the Sierra Nevada takes its name from pioneer lumberman C.B. Shaver (1855-1907), who logged in the area around the turn of the century. In 1893 Shaver built a small rock-filled dam that impounded water to form a small millpond to support logging operations. Shaver Lake was constructed by the Pacific Light & Power Corp., which in 1927 became Southern California Edison.

SHERMAN HEIGHTS
San Diego's first residential subdivision was built on 160-acres of land bought by Captain Matthew Sherman (1827-1898). During the Civil War Sherman served as Lieutenant and later Captain of the 4th Infantry Regiment of the California Volunteers. In 1862 he was stationed in San Diego, and liked it so well that he came back to settle permanently after his discharge from the Army in 1865. Captain Sherman became Customs Collector, a position he held for the next four years. He later served as a City Trustee and then Mayor (1891-92).

SHERMAN OAKS
The San Fernando Valley area is named for "General" Moses Hazeltine Sherman (1853-1932), who came to Los Angeles in 1889 and partnered in building the first interurban streetcar line. He was never in military service, and bestowed "General" on himself, thus engendering confusion between himself and the Civil War hero General William Tecumseh Sherman. In 1902 he was appointed to the first L.A. Water Commission. He later went on to develop the town of Sherman, now West Hollywood, and much of the San Fernando Valley, including Sherman Oaks, named for him.

SILL, MOUNT
One of the twelve fourteen-thousand-foot mountains in the state, it was named for the poet Edward Rowland Sill (1841-1887). A graduate of Yale and the Harvard divinity school, he opted to teach school in his native Cleveland area. Ill health prompted him to move to California where he became principal of Oakland High School, then on to the University of California, where he chaired the English Department from 1874 to 1882. His health failing, he

returned home to Ohio where he died three years later at the age of forty-six. His Berkeley colleague Joseph LeConte bestowed the name to the peak in 1896. It is part of the Palisades of the Sierra Nevada.

SIMEON, SAN

The small town by Hearst Castle on the San Luis Obispo County coastline is next to a state park and state beach of the same name. All refer to Saint Simeon Stylite (390-459), a monk known for his extreme self-mortification, most notably living atop a pillar for thirty-seven years.

SMITH RIVER

The Del Norte County community is bordered by the **Jedediah Smith Redwood State Park.** Established in 1929, this predominately old growth coast redwoods park is bisected by the last major free flowing river in California, the **Smith River.** The park and town are named after the intrepid Jedediah Strong Smith (1799-1831), the first white man to explore the interior of northern California. His journey through the coast redwood belt was part of a remarkable two-year trapping trek which began in 1826. Smith pioneered a trail southwest from the Great Salt Lake across the Mojave Desert through the San Bernardino Mountains into California. Born in a small New York town, he was the leader of a group that used South Pass, in today's Wyoming, for the first east-to-west travel through the Rockies. This would later become the main road for the pioneers who used the Oregon Trail.

SMITH WILDERNESS, DICK

The remote area in the Los Padres National Forest, twelve miles from Santa Barbara, is named for the writer and preservationist Richard J. [Dick] Smith (1920-1977). Born in Minnesota, he came to Santa Barbara County in 1948, where he was hired by the local daily newspaper as Promotion Manager and continued to work there part-time, spending the rest of his time hiking the backcountry. Over the years he came to be known as Santa Barbara County's foremost backwoodsman. He is the co-author of

California Condor: Vanishing American (1964) with Robert O. Easton, and a posthumous work, *Condor Journal: The History, Mythology, and Reality of the California Condor* (1978).

SMITHE REDWOODS STATE NATURAL RESERVE

The northern Mendocino County park contains the 2,000-year-old Frank and Bess Smithe Grove of giant redwoods. The site was formerly a private resort called Land's Redwood Flat. In 1963 it was destined for the loggers' ax, when the Save-the-Redwoods League rallied for funds to buy the property and turn it in to a 665-acre state park.

SOLANO COUNTY

At the request of General Mariano Vallejo, the county was named for Chief Solano (ca 1790-1850) of the Suisunes, a Native American tribe of the region. and a close ally of Vallejo. The Chief was given the Spanish name Francisco Solano during baptism at the Catholic Mission after a celebrated Spanish Franciscan missionary to the Peruvian Indians, later canonized as Saint Francis Solano (1549-1610). Chief Solano applied to the Mexican governor for a land grant for his people. The grant, titled *Suisun Rancho*, was approved and covered most of Suisun Valley. However, the Indians did not fare well in coexistence, and approximately 70,000 of them died in the next three years from a smallpox epidemic brought in by the Russians at Fort Ross. In 1842 the chief sold his grant to Vallejo for $1,000 (which was sold eight years later for $50,000). He and the remainder of his tribe moved to the less colonized Napa area.

SOLEDAD

The Monterey County town grew out of *Misión Nuestra Señora de la Soledad* founded by Father Lasuén in 1791. "Our Most Sorrowful Lady of Solitude" is one of the titles of the Virgin Mary and was instituted to honor her during her solitude on Holy Saturday as she awaited the resurrection of her son.

SOULSBYILLE

Ben Soulsby first settled in this Tuolumne County hamlet in 1853, farming and lumbering on his property. His 12-year-old son, Ben, Jr. (1840-1930), discovered the gold in the area by accident. One evening, while walking the family cow home, he saw some gold, told his father who found a rich vein of ore near the surface of the ground. Young Ben was much excited and wanted to stake a claim at once. However. since he was too young, his father took it up for him. The mine was called the Soulsby Mine. People settled there making a large camp that was later called Soulsbyville. The mine, one of the first hardrock mines in the county, was worked exclusively by Cornish miners. Between sixty and seventy "Cousin Jacks," as they were known, were employed there. It turned out to be the most productive district in the Sierra east gold belt, with a total output value of about $20 million.

STANDISH-HICKEY STATE RECREATION AREA

The park began as a campground acquired by the Save-the-Redwoods League in 1922. In 1950 it became the "Edward Hickey Memorial State Park" in honor of Edward Ritter Hickey, son of a local lumberman who died of influenza while caring for the victims of the 1918 epidemic. It was given its present name in 1953 when additional land was donated by Mr. and Mrs. Miles Standish. Standish, whose family descended directly from the famed pilgrim Miles Standish, grew up in Mendocino County. He and Edward Hickey's father, Henry, were partners in a Mendocino lumber business.

STANDLEY STATE RECREATION AREA, ADMIRAL WILLIAM

Near the headwaters of the south fork of the Eel River in Mendocino County, it was named for a native of those parts, William Harrison Standley (1872-1963) who served from 1933 to his retirement in 1937 as Chief of Naval Operations, the Navy's number one tactical post. He was recalled to active duty in 1941 to serve on the Board of the

Office of Production Management. He also served on the Roberts Commission to investigate the attack on Pearl Harbor. He was Ambassador to the USSR in 1942-1943.

STANFORD
Stanford is the unincorporated area on which Stanford University reposes. It is named not for the Governor and United States senator and "railroad tycoon"—the term usually coupled to his name--but rather for his son, Leland Stanford Jr. (1868-1884), who died at fourteen from typhoid fever. His parents founded the university in 1891 as a memorial to him. Their Victorian mansion in Sacramento is now the **Leland Stanford Mansion State Historic Park.**

STANISLAUS COUNTY
The county is named for the **Stanislaus River**, discovered by Gabriel Moraga in 1806, and renamed *Rio Estanislao* in honor of Estanislao (ca. 1798-1838), a mission-educated renegade Native American chief who led a band of his people in a series of battles against Mexican troops until finally being defeated by General Vallejo in 1826. Estanislao was his baptismal name, the Spanish rendition of Stanislaus, itself the Latin rendition of the name of the 11th century Catholic Saint Stanislav, a bishop of Krakow and martyr regarded as the patron saint of Poland

STANTON
Although there are several stories about how the Orange County town received its name, it is most likely named after real estate developer and politician Philip A. Stanton (1858-1945). He was born in Cleveland, Ohio and came to California in 1887 where he became active in real estate development in Orange County, building Huntington Beach (originally called Pacific City) in 1901 and Seal Beach (initially Bay City) in 1903 and where he made his home. He was invaluable in the community's incorporation in 1911 to prevent the City of Anaheim from building a sewage farm in the community. For many years he was a leader in the state Republican party, serving

as a member of the State Assembly from 1902 to 1910, acting as Speaker in 1909. He was a candidate for the Republican gubernatorial nomination in 1910. In the 1930s he served on the California Highway Commission.

STEVENS PARK
The 22-mile long Santa Clara County creek is named for Elijah Stephens (1797-1883), who settled by Cupertino Creek in 1848, acquiring over two hundred acres of farm land. Born in South Carolina, he had worked as a blacksmith and trapper in the west before heading to California with a wagon train party that came to be known as the Stephens-Townsend-Murphy party. It was the first such group to cross the Sierra. In 1862 he left for Kern County to become the first European-American settler in what is today Bakersfield.

STEVENSON STATE PARK, ROBERT LOUIS
Robert Louis Stevenson (1850-1894), the Scottish author of *Treasure Island* and *Kidnapped,* brought his bride to Silverado in Napa County. He and Fannie Osbourne Stevenson lived there in 1880, from May until July, while he gathered the notes for *Silverado Squatters.* Although nothing remains of Stevenson's cabin, the site is identified on the trail to the summit.

STINSON BEACH
The Marin County beach community is named for the area's largest landowners, Nathan Stinson (1829-1910) and his wife, Rose, who first bought land there in 1866, adding to it until it totaled 16,000 acres, and developing the Willow Camp resort. When the 1906 earthquake brought refugees, they built the first hotel and stores and the first Stinson subdivision was accepted by the County.

Robert F. Stockton

STOCKTON

The city was founded in 1849 by Charles Weber, a German immigrant, the recipient of a Spanish land grant of almost 50,000 acres. A year earlier he had tried prospecting for gold but after a year he concluded that he could find greater success by provisioning the gold-seekers swarming through the area and thus established his town to serve those needs. The name he chose honored the renowned naval officer Commodore Robert Field Stockton (1795-1866) whom he knew and admired. It was the first community in the state to be named for an American, the others being Native American or Spanish.

The New Jersey-born Stockton, the grandson of a signer of the Declaration of Independence, entered the Navy as a midshipman in 1811, in time to see service in the War of 1812. He remained in the Navy for almost forty years, finding action in the Mediterranean and the Caribbean against pirates. In 1845 he was sent to the California coast with 1,500 men and in just a few months he was primarily responsible in taking the state and forming a provisional Unites States government there. After his retirement from the service, he served as a United States Senator from New Jersey. In 1863 he commanded the New Jersey militia when Pennsylvania was invaded by Confederate troops.

SUNOL

The small Alameda County town began as a post office in 1871 on the Mexican land grant known as *Rancho Valle de San José*. It was named in honor of Antonio Suñol (1796-1865), a part owner of the grant. Born in Spain he came to California in 1818, settling in San Jose, where in 1841 he served as *alcalde*.

SUSANA MOUNTAINS, SANTA

Part of the Transverse Ranges, it is unclear when and how it was named, most likely it honors the third-century virgin and martyr Saint Susanna,, said to have been the daughter of Saint Gabinius. She was beheaded about 295 at the command of the Roman emperor Diocletian, in her father's house. **Santa Susana Pass State Historic Park** is located at the juncture of the Simi Hills and the Santa Susana Mountains.

SUSANVILLE

The town was named in 1857 for Susan Roop (1841-1921), daughter of Isaac Roop, an early settler who had come to California in 1840 from Maryland, a widower with three children, settling in the Honey Lake valley where he built up his holding and launched the village of Rooptown which he would later name after his daughter. In 1858 Roop became the first territorial governor of the provisional Nevada Territory. In 1865 he returned to Susanville where his daughter had settled and married. There, he became Lassen County's district attorney for two terms and stayed in the town that he had built and loved until his death. Susan resided in the town as well until her own death in 1921, and both were buried in the town's cemetery..

SUTTER COUNTY

One of the original twenty-seven counties of the state, it was named after John Augustus Sutter (1803-1880). Born in Germany of parents who had originally come from Switzerland, he immigrated to America at twenty-one. He settled in Missouri for a few years, working as a trader on the Santa Fe Trail, before deciding in 1839 to try his luck in California.. He received permission from the Mexican government to establish a 50,000-acre settlement along the Sacramento River, near present-day Sacramento, but then occupied solely by Native Americans, and which he would name New Helvetia. There he built **Sutter's Fort** (now a State Park). In 1842 he enlarged his settlement by purchasing Fort Ross in the Sacramento Valley after the Russians had abandoned it. In a short time he had what amounted to a private kingdom and Sutter's Fort became a regular stop for the increasing number of pioneers coming to California and provided him with skein of relationships that offered some political protection when the United States seized control of California in 1846. Unfortunately, just as the war ended, something occurred that would destroy all his achievements: On January 24, 1858, James Marshall, a carpenter hired by Sutter to build a sawmill upstream on the American River near Coloma, discovered some gold nuggets there. He took them to Sutter who beseeched his employees to keep the finding secret. But, in a few months' time, the word was out and the Gold Rush started. All of a sudden, Sutter's workmen left him for the gold fields. Squatters swarmed over his land, devastating crops and butchering his herds. By 1852, New Helvetia had been destroyed and Sutter was moneyless. He would spend the remainder of his life in pursuit of compensation from the government, both state and federal, and would die a disappointed man. The Amador County community of **Sutter Creek** is also named for him.

T

TAFT

The city situated in a small valley in the southern foothills of the Temblor Mountain Range in Kern County is named after the nation's twenty-seventh President, William Howard Taft (1857-1930). He had nothing to do with the town; it seems that in the 1920s, much of it was devastated by fire and the citizens wanted to rename it—at the time it bore the unfortunate name of Moron. According to legend, at a meeting of community leaders gathered to come up with a new name, Taft was suggested as his picture hung on a calendar on display at the Post Office where the meeting was held. Taft was not only President (1909-1913), but a Chief Justice of the United States (1921-1930).

TAYLOR STATE PARK, SAMUEL P.

The namesake of the west Marin County park of almost 3,000 acres, Samuel Penfield Taylor (1827-1886), set sail for California in a schooner he bought with a group of friends in that *annus mirabilus*, 1849. Meeting with some success in the gold fields he used his money to purchase 200 acres in western Marin County and built the first paper mill on the west coast. The little town of Taylorville grew around it. He also built Camp Taylor, California's first site for recreational camping, becoming one of the most popular weekend recreation areas during the late 1870s and early 1880s. The mill and resort eventually closed down and the state took the property in 1945 for non-payment of taxes.

TEMPLETON

The San Luis Obispo County community was founded in 1886 when the West Coast Land Company laid out 150 acres south of Paso Robles as a town to be called "Crocker." It was named for Charles F. Crocker, the son of the famous San Francisco railroad (Southern Pacific) and banking magnate. Charles F. (known as "Fred") was a vice president of Southern Pacific and part owner of the West Coast Land Company. There are at least three theories as to why the name was changed to Templeton. The first is that it was discovered that there was already a town by that name, so it was changed to honor Charles' son, [Charles] Templeton Crocker (1884-1948), though research shows that there was no other California town by that name. The second theory is that the lots were not selling because of Crocker's reputation as a less than fair businessman. Locals distrusted him and the Southern Pacific Railroad. So the name was changed. Finally, there is the story put out by the Templeton Historical Museum Society that Crocker modestly declined the honor of having a town named after him and chose the name of his two-year-old son instead. Whichever is true, young Templeton would grow up to become the epitome, wrote Kevin Starr, of "the clubby, almost inbred life characteristic of provincial urban elites in the United States prior to the Second World War." He went to Yale before returning to San Francisco to build a 118-acre estate in Hillsborough, He collected rare books, wrote the lyrics for an opera, and re-founded the California Historical Society. When the Depression hit, he decided to ride it out on a fabulous yacht he had built, sailing around the world. He returned to San Francisco to manage the St. Francis Hotel which the Crockers had built.

THORNTON STATE BEACH

Robert S. Thornton (1817-18??) of Rhode Island, a blacksmith, arrived in the San Francisco area in 1851 after enduring a grueling 17,000-mile, 8-month sea voyage. When he heard that the old Spanish land grants at the north end of San Mateo County were being opened to settlers, he established a claim to part of the area south of Lake Merced near the ocean. This became the State Beach bearing his name. He is credited with being the first resident of Daly City.

TILDEN REGIONAL PARK

The 2,000-plus-acre park above Berkeley is named for East Bay financier Charles Lee Tilden (1857-1950), first president of the East Bay Regional Park District Board of Directors. The son of a judge, he was born in the Sierra foothills town of Chile Gulch in Calaveras County. The family moved to San Francisco when he was eight. A graduate of Berkeley (1878) and Hastings College of Law (1881), he was active with the California National Guard, serving in the Spanish American War, and retired with the rank of major--and was usually referred to thereafter as "Major C. L. Tilden." He practiced law in San Francisco after the war, then made his home in Alameda, where he was involved in various ventures. Beside serving on the Park board, he was a trustee of Mills College.

TORRANCE

Jared S. Torrance (1852-1921) came to southern California around 1887 from New York. He became vice president of Union Oil and its subsidiary Union Tool Company. In 1912 he persuaded Union Tool to purchase land from the Dominguez Estate Company and create an industrial town based on the garden-city concept. He hired the famous landscape architect Frederick Law Olmsted, Jr. to design the community which would take Torrance's name. Unfortunately, the concept did not catch on. Much of the employment initially offered was too sporadic to inspire workers to make long-term investments in houses. The town also met resistance from labor leaders who saw the project as an attempt to control non-union workers. As a consequence most Union Tool employees chose to live outside the town and commute to work on the Pacific Electric cars. In 1922, the city had only 2,500 residents, far fewer than planned. Only after Torrance shed its model industrial city image did its population significantly grow.

TORREY PINES STATE NATURAL RESERVE
Located within San Diego city limits, it takes its name from the Torrey pine trees preserved there, "officially" discovered by Dr. Charles Christopher Parry in 1850 who was in the area as botanist for the U.S.-Mexico Boundary Survey. He named them for his former instructor at Columbia University, John Torrey (1796-1873), one of the foremost botanists of his day. Torrey himself never came to California. The area was first preserved as a city park in 1899 and over the years grew to over a thousand acres in size, becoming a State Park in 1959. Adjacent to the park is **Torrey Pines State Beach**.

TRACY
Tracy traces its beginnings to 1878 with the construction of a new rail line that started in Oakland and circled the shores of San Francisco Bay, through Martinez to connect to a point near the base of the Altamont Pass, an ideal location as a transit hub. As J.H. Stewart, the Central Pacific Railroad's superintendent, had great respect for Lathrop J. Tracy, an Ohio merchant, he honored his friend and mentor by naming the town after him.

TRAVIS AIR FORCE BASE
Located a few miles east of Fairfield in Solano County, the base, formerly known as Fairfield-Suisun Air Force base, was renamed in 1951 in honor of Brigadier General Robert F. Travis (1904-1950), who was killed when a B-29 crashed on August 5, 1950. The ensuing fire caused the bombs in the bay to detonate about fifteen minutes after impact, killing General Travis and eighteen others. Although the

aircraft was carrying a nuclear weapon, the bomb's plutonium pit was not installed, rendering it harmless.

TRUCKEE
The name of the Sierra Nevada town and the river derives from a Paiute Indian guide who, in 1844, assisted thousands of emigrants migrating west across the Humboldt Sink. His name sounded like "Tro-kay" to the white men, who dubbed him "Truckee." He became a favorite of the settlers who found him to be honest and helpful. Chief Truckee fought bravely alongside Col. John C. Frémont in the Mexican War and was the father of Chief Winnemucca.

TWAIN HARTE
In 1924 the Tuolomne County resort community was christened Twain Harte after the two most famous Mother Lode authors, Mark Twain (1835-1910) and Bret Harte (1836-1902). Twain lived in San Francisco during the 1860s and it was there he achieved his first success with his famous tale of the jumping frog. Harte moved to California from his native Albany, New York in 1853. He worked various jobs, including journalism, finally achieving success in San Francisco with his short stories about Gold Rush days and editing *The Overland Monthly*. He left California permanently in 1871 to pursue his literary ambitions.

TUSTIN
The Orange County city was established as a real estate venture by Columbus Tustin (1826-1873). Born in Philadelphia, his family moved to Petaluma where he and a partner went into the carriage manufacturing business. Looking for other prospects in 1868 he ventured to southern California where the *ranchos* were being divided and sold. They were able to buy 1300 acres of the *Rancho Santiago de Santa Ana*. Over the next four years Tustin set about establishing "Tustin City" on his share of the parcel. He laid the streets out through the wild mustard and sycamore trees that covered the area. He started selling lots

and established the school district and the post office. When sales flagged, he offered lots free to anyone who would build a home. In 1877 Tustin competed unsuccessfully with Santa Ana for the southern terminus of the Southern-Pacific Railroad, thereby sealing the fate of his "city": Tustin would remain a small town, Santa Ana would become a city. At his death, Columbus Tustin was a a bitterly disappointed man. Nonetheless, with the abundance of water, the community named after him gradually became established as an agricultural center.

V

VACAVILLE

Juan Manuel Vaca left New Mexico with the Rowland-Workman expedition, the first group of emigrants to enter California by traveling on the Old Spanish Trail. While most of the party remained in southern California, Vaca, along with Juan Felipe Peña, had the good fortune of meeting Governor Manuel Vallejo who told them of the fertile Lagoon Valley between modern-day Fairfield and Vacaville in Solano County and promised them if they would settle there and raise crops and livestock, he would grant them the land. When they had satisfied the requirements, they were granted ten square leagues—44,384 acres—an expanse encompassing all of Lagoon Valley and stretching into what is now Yolo County.. In 1850 Vaca sold a square English league of his land (about nine square miles) to William McDaniel for $3,000, with the provision that one square mile be laid out as a new town of Vacaville.

VALLEJO

Solano County's largest city's was once part of the 84,000-acre *Rancho Suscol,* a Mexican land grant of 1843 owned by General Mariano Guadalupe Vallejo (1808-1890). A native Californian, he joined the Mexican army when he was seventeen and rose to the highest military post in northern California. He was responsible for military peace in the region until 1846, when independence-minded Californians rose up against the Mexican government in the Bear Flag Revolt, and the annexation of California to the United States. Though a Mexican army officer, he acquiesced to the annexation, recognizing the greater resources of the United States and benefits that would bring to California.. In 1850, he proposed plans for a new city, to be called *Eureka,* with the capitol, university, botanical garden and other features. After a state wide referendum, his proposal was accepted, although a new name was decided upon: *Vallejo.*

VAN DAMME STATE PARK

A few miles south of the town of Mendocino, the park was named for Charles G. Van Damme (1873-1930) who was born at nearby Little River, the son of early settlers of the region who had emigrated from Belgium. Van Damme became a successful business man, operating the Richmond-San Rafael ferry line, Remembering fondly the land of his childhood, he bought a plot along the redwood coast. Upon his death, he willed it to the State Park system, the park opening in 1934.

Hoyt S. Vandenberg

VANDENBURG AIR FORCE BASE

The base, near Lompoc in Santa Barbara County, was originally built in 1941 as the Army's Camp Cooke. It was transferred to the Air Force in 1957 and evolved into a space and ballistic missile test facility. In 1958 the name was changed to honor General Hoyt S. Vandenberg (1899-1954), the second Chief of Staff of the Air Force, a pioneer in moving the Air Force into missile and space operations. He had a distinguished career, serving as commanding general of the Ninth Air Force during World War II and Director of the Central Intelligence Agency.

VAN NUYS

Los Angeles' San Fernando Valley district is named for an early settler, Isaac Newton Van Nuys (1835-1912), a native of West Sparta, New York, who at thirty moved to California where he teamed up with his father-in-law, Isaac Lankershim, and others to form the first large-scale wheat operation in southern California. At his death, the new town of Van Nuys was named in his honor.

VENTURA

The name of the city and county is an abbreviated form of "San Buenaventura," the name of the mission established by Fr. Junípero Serra in 1782. It had been planned as the third in the chain of Missions, but was destined to be the ninth and last founded during his lifetime. The eponymous Italian saint--known in English as Saint Bonaventure (1221-1274)--was a contemporary of Saint Thomas Aquinas and, like him, a leading scholar and theologian of his time. A Doctor of the Church, the Franciscan priest served as Cardinal-Bishop of Albano and Minister General of the Friars Minor. He was canonized in 1482.

VERDUGO

In reward for his services as a soldier in the California military, José María Verdugo, (1751-1831), who served many years as a guard at the San Gabriel Mission, was given the first private land grant of California, the *Rancho San Rafael*. It spanned 36,000 acres of grazing land and included what is today called the **Verdugo Mountains**. In 1798 he retired from the military to devote himself full-time to ranching. His route to and from Los Angeles at his property's southern edge came to be known as Verdugo Road and is now the Glendale community of Montrose-**Verdugo City**. At his death, Verdugo left his vast property to his son Julio and daughter Catalina. Over the ensuing years the family's fortunes declined, causing them to sell or mortgage parts of their property.

VICTORVILLE

In about 1885, the community was known simply as "Victor" in honor of Jacob Nash Victor (1835-1907), a construction superintendent for the California Southern Railroad. It was established as a result of the original railroad station constructed approximately one mile northwest of the narrows of the Mojave River. Victor's major accomplishment was providing a Pacific Coast terminal for the second transcontinental railroad in the United States. He guided the reconstruction of 30 miles of washed-out track from Fallbrook to San Diego, then cut through the Southern Pacific tracks at Colton. In 1885 he drove the first engine through Cajón Pass, signaling linkage of San Bernardino and Barstow, and completion of the transcontinental route. In 1901 the community's name was changed by the United States Post Office from "Victor" to "Victorville" due to the confusion associated with the community of Victor, Colorado

VISALIA

When California became a state in 1850 Tulare County did not exist. The land that now constitutes the county was part of Mariposa County. In 1852 some pioneers settled in this area, and petitioned the state legislature for county status. On July 10 of that year Tulare County became a reality. One of the first inhabitants of a fort built by the settlers was Nathaniel Vise, who surveyed the new settlement. It--the oldest town between San Francisco and Los Angeles--was named for his home town, Visalia, Kentucky, established by, and named for, his father.

VIZCAINO, CAPE

The Mendocino promontory was named by the U.S. Coast and Geodetic Survey to honor the Spanish explorer Sebastián Vizcaíno (1548-1624), who sighted the cape in 1603. Born into a merchant family in Spain, at thirty-eight he went to New Spain, then on to the Philippines for three years, before settling in Mexico City. In 1601 he was commissioned to lead an expedition to find a safe harbor in Alta California for Spanish ships to use on their return voyage from Manila. The following year he entered and named San Diego Bay, then sailed up the coast naming most of the prominent features. With his mission accomplished, he returned to Mexico City and, in 1607, was appointed General of the Manila Galleons. In 1610 he was named Spain's first Ambassador to Japan. In 1614 he retired to Spain, but was recalled to sail to Acapulco and repel a Dutch invasion. He was appointed *alcalde* of that city, a position he occupied for five years, before finally retiring to Mexico City.

W

WALKER PASS

Born in Tennessee, Joseph Rutherford Walker (1798-1876) grew to be a powerful mountain man and trail blazer, helped establish the Santa Fe trail, and discovered "Walker Pass," the gap in the Sierra Nevada Mountains. He was the first white man to find the Yosemite Valley in California. Walker spent about twelve years as a trapper in the far west. He headed west with Captain Benjamin Bonneville to lead an expedition to California that left Green River in Wyoming in July of 1833 and arrived on the Pacific coast in November of that same year. Walker also served as John Frémont's guide on his expedition in 1845. Later Walker served as an Army scout and also prospected. Frémont not only named the pass after Walker, but also the **Walker River** and **Walker Lake**. Walker Pass was designated a National Register Property and National Historic Landmark in 1961.

WARNER SPRINGS

When he was twenty-three Jonathan Trumbull Warner (1807-1890) left his Lyme, Connecticut home for St. Louis to sign on with an expedition led by famed mountain-man Jedediah Smith. He ended up in Los Angeles where he soon married a young English woman who had been raised as the ward of the widowed mother of Pío Pico, who would later become governor of Alta California. Warner became a Mexican citizen and in 1844 applied for, and was awarded, the 48,000-acre *Rancho Valle de San José y Agua Caliente* in San Diego, which included a hot springs.. He changed its name to Warner's Ranch—and while he was at it—his name to Juan José Warner. He set up a trading post on the land—the sole rest stop between New Mexico and Los Angeles for wagon trains, settlers, and gold-seekers. General Kearny passed there in 1846 and the Mormon Battalion in 1847. The first Butterfield Stage stopped at this ranch on October 6, 1858, on its 2,600-mile, 24-day trip from Tipton, Missouri to San Francisco, the southern overland route into California. This property was listed in the National Register of Historic Places in 1966.

In 1851 the ranch was attacked by Cahuilla Indians, who stole the livestock, and burned down Warner's house and trading post. Ruined, he left for Los Angeles, never to return. He took an active part in politics after the American occupancy of California. In 1852 he represented San Diego County in the Senate. In 1860 he was elected to the Assembly. In his latter years he was generally known as Col. J. J. Warner.

WASHINGTON, MOUNT

It is thought by many that Mt. Washington in northeast Los Angeles was named after the nation's first president Rather, it was named for Colonel Henry Washington, who. on November 7, 1852, under contract with the United States Surveyor General for California, surveyed the San Bernardino Base Line and Meridian from a point just west of Mount San Bernardino, at an elevation of 10,300 feet, east of present day Highland. The Base and Meridian lines serve as the initial surveying point (known as the "point of beginning") for all of Southern California). During the Civil War he served as aide-de-camp to General J.E.B. Magruder. In 1909 the Mt. Washington area was developed into an exclusive residential site.

WATSONVILLE
Mission lands in the Pajaro Valley, about five miles from Monterey Bay, were granted to Mexican citizens, one of whom was Sebastián Rodriquez, who obtained the *Rancho Bolsa de Pajaro*. John H. Watson (18??-1882) arrived in 1851 and filed a claim against Rodriquez. Watson lost and, after several years, moved on to Nevada. Just how the town came to be named after him is not at all clear. What is known about the man is that he had served in the California State Assembly (1849-50), prior to which he had been appointed the first district judge of the Third Judicial District, which included the counties of Contra Costa, Santa Clara, Santa Cruz, and Monterey.

WATTS
Some time during the 1880's this small parcel of land in what is today called South Central Los Angeles was purchased by Charles H. Watts, a Pasadena developer. In 1907 it was incorporated as a separate city, named after Watts. It voted to annex itself to Los Angeles in 1926. It is the home of **Watts Tower of Simon Rodia State Historic Park.**

WEAVERVILLE
Little is known about John Weaver, the man for whom the Trinity County seat was named, other than that he had been prospecting for gold in the area in 1849, then disappeared. A year later, when the first cabins were being built in the Weaver Creek Basin, settlers felt that the area needed a name. The first choice was "Weaver," but the name was being used elsewhere in California. "Weaver City" didn't suit either so they went with "Weavertown." When they found out that the latter was taken they changed it to "Weaverville." The oldest continuously used

220

Chinese temple in California is preserved at the **Weaverville Joss House State Historic Park.**

WEED
On the western slopes of Mount Shasta, the Siskiyou County town is named for Abner E. Weed (1842-1917). Born in Penobscot County, Maine, he left home at twenty-one to enlist in the Union Army and was present at Lee's surrender in Appomattox. Soon after his return home, he lighted out for California, spending about twenty years around Truckee, logging in the winters during that period. In 1889 he moved to the Sisson (Mt. Shasta City) area where he opened and operated two saw mills--the Weed Lumber Co.—which was the beginning of the town and at their height produced 60,000 feet of lumber a day. In 1905 he sold the company to the Long-Bell Lumber Company for an estimated two million dollars. With some of the profits he bought large tracts of land in Klamath County, Oregon, a ranch in Contra Costa County, as well as 11,000 acres in Siskiyou County. He also served in the State Senate and on the Siskiyou County Board of Supervisors.

WHITNEY, MOUNT
In July, 1864, the members of the California Geological Survey named the tallest peak in the "Lower 48" after Josiah Whitney (1819-1896), the State Geologist of California, and benefactor of the Survey and professor of geology at Harvard. He was appointed to conduct the survey in 1860, but did not complete his work until 1874, after which he returned to Harvard where he remained for the rest of his career.

WHITTIER
In 1887 a group of Quakers interested in starting up a community in California acquired about 1300 acres as the "Pickering Land and Water Development Company." Many "Friends" on the East Coast bought lots from the Company, sight unseen, but all "fair-minded people" were invited to settle there. The town was named after fellow Quaker John Greenleaf Whittier, the famous New

England poet, writer and newspaper editor. Whittier never had the opportunity to visit the town that bears his name but he did write and dedicate a poem in its honor:

"My Name I Give To Thee"
Dear Town, for whom the flowers are born,
Stars shine, and happy songbirds sing,
What can my evening give to thy morn,
My Winter to Thy Spring? A life not
    void of pure intent
With small desert of praise or blame;
The Love I felt, the Good I meant,
  I leave Thee with My Name.

WILDER RANCH STATE PARK

The Connecticut-born Deloss D. Wilder (1826-1906) came to California in 1850 with the intention of mining for gold. He tried his luck in Placer County. but without much success. The following year he settled in Marin County, where, with $200 in savings, he started a small dairy farm. It became profitable and ten years later he moved to the Santa Cruz area where he bought a large tract a few miles from town and established the Wilder Dairy Ranch which remained in his family for five generations until 1969 when property taxes exceeded income. In 1974 the State acquired the land to preserve its natural environment. Today Wilder Ranch State Park comprises almost 7,000 acres of coastal wetlands.

WILDOMAR

Situated in southwest Riverside County, the town was founded in 1886 with, as with so many other communities, the establishment of a Post Office. The name "Wildomar" was coined from the names of its three founders: WILliam Collier, DOnald Graham and MARgaret Collier.

WILLIAMS

William H. Williams (1828-1909) was born in Maryland, moved as a child with his family to Ohio, then to Illinois.

In 1850 he and a trio of companions left home for the gold fields by covered wagon. He tried different vocations for a couple of years before deciding to farm at Spring Valley. Within seven years he had managed to acquire over 7,000 acres of land and over a thousand sheep. In 1876, knowing the railroad was coming through his property, he began selling lots ten miles west of Colusa, the county seat. By the time he railroad reached the town, the area was booming. Initially called "Central," it was soon changed to honor its founder who built a large residence and a grain warehouse there.

WILLIAMSON, MOUNT
California's second highest mountain (14,389 feet), located about six miles north of its highest mountain, Mount Whitney, is named for Robert Stockton Williamson (1824-1882). After graduating from West Point in 1848, he was assigned to the Army's topographical engineers and took part in various surveys in California until 1856. After the Civil War he was chief topographical engineer of the Department of the Pacific. In 1869 he was promoted to Lieutenant-Colonel.

WILLITS
The "Gateway to the Redwoods" in Mendocino County was founded by Hiram Willits (1821-1882). Born on a farm in Indiana, he moved with his parents when he was twenty-one to Van Buren County, Iowa. In 1850 he and his wife trekked across the plains to California. After a few years farming and operating a "public house" in Colusa County, he bought some land in Little Lake Valley in Mendocino County. Gradually he began to sell off town lots from his farm, and as settlers began to arrive, the store and blacksmith had about all the patronage they could handle. The hamlet took on the name of its founder, and "Willitsville" showed up on local maps. Willits was the first postmaster of the town and later became a successful breeder of race horses. In 1888, with the advent of the railroad, Willitsville incorporated with a population of 720 and shortened its name to Willits.

WILMINGTON

The Los Angeles district next to the port of San Pedro was named by its developer, Phineas Banning, for his hometown of Wilmington, Delaware, which, in turn, was presumably named for British statesman Spencer Compton, First Earl of Wilmington (1673-1743).

WILSON, MOUNT

The Tennessee-born fur trapper Benjamin D. Wilson (1811-1878) first set foot in California in 1841 with the intention of continuing on to China, but liked what he saw and stayed on. Five years later he joined up to fight in the Mexican War, was captured, and spent the remainder of the conflict as a prisoner. After the war he went into business in Los Angeles and was eventually elected its second mayor in 1851. He subsequently served as a County Supervisor and was elected to three terms of the State Senate. In 1854 he bought a 128-acre ranch near present day San Gabriel and lived there until his death. Don Benito, as he was known, needed lumber for his fences and wine barrels. He had been informed that the mountain peak that loomed above his ranch held forests of sugar pine and cedar. To get that timber, Wilson built in 1864 the first modern trail up the peak. He found two cabin ruins already there, possibly built by horse thieves of an earlier time. The timber on Mount Wilson, as the mountain became known, apparently didn't suit Wilson's needs. A few weeks later he abandoned the venture. But his trail remained, and for many years was the only pathway to the mountain top.

Theodore Winters

WINTERS
In 1848 the father and siblings of Theodore Winters (1823-1906) left their home in Illinois for California via the Oregon Trail, leaving him to dispose of the family business. The following year he joined them at Forest City on the American River, where they had set up a hauling business. When gold was discovered in Nevada they began hauling freight from Placerville into the Carson Valley. They grew rich from the business as well as from interests they held in the Comstock Lode. With their wealth they started buying land and by 1867 Winters owned more than 18,000 acres. About 1860 Winters began to interest himself in horse racing and built a race track in Carson Valley. He is credited with introducing thoroughbred horses to the west. The climate at Carson Valley proved to be severe in the winter months, so in 1865 he bought 1300 acres of land in Yolo County and constructed race tracks on both sides of Putah Creek. He commuted between his ranches. Realizing that the proposed construction of a railroad north from Vacaville would benefit him, not only in shipping agricultural products, but also in moving his horses to race tracks. This prompted him to sell the land to the Vaca Valley Railroad for $5000, along with substantial money to build the bridge across Putah Creek. This was the beginning of the town of Winters that would be

225

developed by the railroad.

In 1890 Winters ran for governor of Nevada and sold all of his property in Winters, both to help finance his campaign and also to move his horses to Nevada where his opponent couldn't claim that he was a "carpetbagger." He was soundly beaten in the election that fall. That political race was the turning point in Winters' fortunes. The campaign left him heavily in debt, and he had to sell some of his Nevada property. Financial problems added to his misfortune He died at his home in the Carson Valley.

WOOD STATE BEACH, EMMA

Emma Wood (1884-1944) acquired large land holdings on the coast and coastal slope of north Ventura County known as "Taylor's Ranch," land that was originally part of *Rancho San Miguelito*. In the late 1950s her husband and heir donated to the state the slice of oceanfront property south of the ranch now known as Emma Wood Beach. Wood was the granddaughter of Green B. Taylor, the original owner of the 30,000-acre Taylor Ranch. He had brought his family by covered wagon from Tennessee. He ran sheep on the land until his death near the turn of the twentieth century.

WOODSON BRIDGE STATE RECREATION AREA

The Tehama Count woodland park is situated along the Sacramento River between Chico and Red Bluff. The Woodson Bridge was named after Warren Nicholas Woodson (1863-1951). A native of Sacramento, he had moved to Red Bluff where he became its postmaster and had the idea of developing land in nearby Corning. In the 1890s he started the Maywood Colony, one of the largest real estate speculations of its time. In December, 1920, the board of supervisors honored Woodson by naming the new bridge being built across the Sacramento River at Squaw Hill the "Woodson Bridge." The State of California built a park which was named for the bridge in 1964.

WRIGHT, MOUNT CEDRIC

The only two photographers who have had California mountains named for them were also best of friends. One was Ansel Adams. The other was Cedric Wright (1889-1959), a photographer of unusual experience. He started life as a violinist, studying for six years at Prague and Vienna, teaching the instrument at Mills College and the University of California Extension. In middle age when, because of arthritic fingers, he had to give up music; he turned to nature photography. In 1961 the U.S. Board of Geographic Names named a 12,372-foot mountain in Kings Canyon National Park for Wright whom it characterized as "an internationally known photographer whose photography has made a significant contribution to the appreciation of the natural scene."

WRIGHTWOOD

Between 1886 and 1926 the Swarthout Valley in San Bernardino County was homesteaded by many men, among them Sumner Banks Wright (1866-1944), who gave his name to the town. Born in Columbus, Ohio, he came as a small boy with his family to California in 1870, settling in the San Bernardino area. In 1890 he bought forty acres, planted apple orchards, introduced cattle ranching to the valley, and eventually expanded his holdings to 3,300 acres. He established the thousand-head Circle Mountain Ranch at the eastern end of the valley which he operated during the early 1900s. In 1924 Wright subdivided his property into lots for home sites. Later, he would lose all his property to the bank after numerous legal battles and move to Colton.

Y

YNEZ, SANTA

The anglicized name "Santa Ynez" was derived from Mission Santa Inés, established in 1804, the first Spanish settlement in that area of Santa Barbara County. It was named in honor of Saint Agnes, the fourth-century virgin and martyr who endured many trials and tortures, and was finally beheaded in 354. The town, the valley, and **Santa Ynez Peak** take their names from the mission.

YORBA LINDA

The name Yorba dates back as far as 1769 when José Antonio Yorba (1743-1825) was part of an expedition exploring the area that would be Orange County. Yorba was born in a village near Barcelona and had no formal education, remaining illiterate throughout his life. He joined the Spanish army and was shipped out to New Spain, where he eventually became one of the military escorts who accompanied Father Junípero Serra at the time of his founding of the Franciscan missions. Upon his discharge from the army in 1809, he received his land grant of 62,000 acres of land, which came to be known as *Rancho*

Santiago de Santa Ana. Over the years portions were sold off; in 1907 Jacob Stern, a Fullerton resident, sold a large area to the Janss Corporation, which subdivided it and named the new town "Yorba Linda." The second part of the name is Spanish for "beautiful."

YOUNTVILLE

George Calvert Yount (1794-1865) was born in North Carolina, then moved with his parents to Missouri, before going out on his own to California as a trapper. In 1831 he became the first European-American to settle in the Napa Valley. Five years later he obtained a land grant, the first one to be awarded to an American citizen in northern California. Yount named his land *Caymus Rancho* after a tribe of Native Americans in the area. It was there, in the early 1850s, that he laid out the town's first boundaries. which he named Sebastopol, notwithstanding that there was already a town over the hill with the same name. Two years after his death, in 1867, the town was renamed Yountville in his honor. He has the distinction of having planted the first grape vines in Napa Valley.

YSIDRO, SAN

The community annexed by the city of San Diego in 1957 is named for the Spanish Saint Isidore the Farmer (1070-1130), sometimes known as Saint Isidore the Laborer. He was a farm worker known for his devotion and certain "miracles" that happened around him. He was married to a real saint, a canonized saint known as Santa María de la Cabeza.

Z

ZABRISKIE POINT

As well as being the title of a 1970 film by Italian director Michelangelo Antonioni, Zabriskie Point is an elevated overlook of a landscape of gullies and mud hills at the edge of the Funeral Mountains, a few miles from the edge of Death Valley. It is named for Christian Brevoort Zabriskie (1864-1936). He was born at Fort Bridger in the Wyoming Territory, where his father, an Army captain, was stationed. When he was twenty-one he met borax magnate F.M. "Borax" Smith who hired him to supervise several hundred Chinese laborers of the Pacific Coast Borax Company near Candelaria, Nevada. This was the beginning of a life-long career in the borax industry.. He ultimately became vice president and general manager of the company and served in that capacity for thirty-six years until his retirement in 1933. During this time, the company had phased out most of its operations in Nevada but had moved on to greater production in the Death Valley area. The company established and aggressively developed the famous Twenty Mule Team Borax trademark in order to promote the sale of its product. The name derived from the twenty-mule teams that were used to transport borax out of Death Valley in the 1880s.

Z'BERG SUGAR PINE POINT STATE BEACH, ED

The park was named for Sacramento-born Edwin L. Z'berg (19??-1975) in recognition of his contributions to the improvement of the state park system. While serving in the State Assembly (1958-1975) he actively promoted such environmental legislation as the federal Tahoe Regional Planning Agency, Tahoe Preservation Act, and the Forest Practice Act. A champion of efforts to preserve and protect Lake Tahoe, Sugar Pine Point State Park on the west shore of Lake Tahoe was a favorite of Z'bergs.

ZMUDOWSKI STATE BEACH

The 220-acre Zmudowski (pronounced Mud-ow-ski) State Beach was named for the Pajaro Valley family that first acquired the land soon after California became a state. It was donated in 1950 by Mary Zmudowski, a Watsonville school teacher for more than fifty years. It included 9,124 feet of ocean frontage. In 1952 the Park Commission changed the name of the Monterey County park from Pajaro River to Zmudowski to recognize the contribution of her family.